TEACHING VALUES

TEACHING VALUES

Critical Perspectives
on Education, Politics, and Culture

Ron Scapp

RoutledgeFalmer
NEW YORK AND LONDON

Published in 2003 by
Routledge
29 West 35th Street
New York, NY 10001
www.routledge-ny.com

Published in Great Britain by
Routledge
11 New Fetter Lane
London EC4P 4EE
www.routledge.co.uk

Routledge is an imprint of the Taylor & Francis Group.
Printed in the United States of America on acid-free paper.
Design and typography: Jack Donner

10 9 8 7 6 5 4 3 2 1

Library of Congress Cataloging-in-Publication Data

Scapp, Ron, 1955–
   Teaching values : education, politcs, and culture / Ron Scapp
      p.   cm.
   Includes bibliographical references and index.
   ISBN 0-415-93106-1 – ISBN 0-415-93107-X (pbk)
      1. Moral Education—United States. 2. Values—United States. 3. Multi-
cultural education—United States. 4. Critical pedagogy—United States. I.
Title.

LC311 .S32 2002
370.11'4—dc21   2002069727

*In gratitude to all those
who have taught me values—
in and out of the classroom—
intentionally and not.*

Contents

Acknowledgments   **ix**

Introduction   **1**

1. **When the Truth Is Gone**   19
   Teaching in an Age of Uncertainty

2. **Happy to Be Nappy**   41

3. **From Substandard to Nonstandard English**   65
   Getting beyond the Morality of Speaking Right

4. **Go Tell it on the Mount**   89

5. **But Is He Straight?**   109
   Identity, Teaching, and the Simple Acts of Privilege

6. **Why Multiculturalism (*Still*)?**   133

Epilogue   **161**
Teaching in an Extra-Moral Sense

Bibliography   **179**

Index   **185**

Acknowledgments

I would like to thank my students and colleagues at the College of Mount Saint Vincent for their input and support of my work in general and this book in particular. My colleagues Ed Meyer, Rita Dytell, Barbara Cohen, Barbara Smith, Susan Apold, Sister Margaret Egan, Barbara Shimmel, Sister Anne Denise Brennan, Kathleen Schmalz, and especially Lizzette Zayas and Evelyn Lopez have in different ways offered support and advice regarding my work as director of the Graduate Program in Urban and Multicultural Education at the college and have had an influence on the direction of this book.

My thanks to the many people at the United Federation of Teachers, particularly Aminda Gentile and Barbara Tubertina, director and coordinator, respectively, of the New York City Teacher Center, for their generosity and the resulting collaborative projects. Thanks also to the members of the New York State United Teachers and the Teacher Center/ Institutions of Higher Education Advisory Committee, especially Lynn VanEseltine and Deborah Thomas, for all their support.

I am grateful for the enthusastic support offered by Enora Brown a few years back and the continued support of Kenneth Saltman. I am particularly grateful to Robin Truth Goodman for all that she has heard and commented on. I thank Susan Bordo for our ongoing, if sporadic, conversations concerning philosophy and culture, and Alphonso Lingis, David B. Allison,

Allen S. Weiss, and David F. Krell for embracing my work and encouraging me to do what I do. I am also very thankful for discussions with Stephen Steinberg.

I would also like to thank those at the Danforth Foundation for their support early on in my career, as well as the Chaney, Goodman, and Schwerner Scholarship. I will be forever grateful to Harvey Burstein and Kathleen Brogan.

Finally, I wish to express my deepest appreciation to Kevin MacDonald, Brian Seitz, Tod Mijanovich (Group Thought), Steven F. Kruger, Gloria Watkins, Virginia Ben Ayoun, and Meryl Siegman for all that you have done in the name of friendship and love.

Introduction

For years now there have been numerous debates and some bitter fights over the question of values in the United States. From abortion to equal rights for lesbians and gays, from environmentalism to globalism, from the legacy of slavery to the consequences of immigration, many, if not all, dimensions of contemporary American life have been advocated or rejected based on a call to arms concerning the values being advanced or abandoned. What has apparently complicated, if not defined, these debates and fights is the diversity of the cultures and people involved. Thus the issue of values is made more problematic by the myriad communities claiming moral standing and knowledge. Add to the mix postmodernism with its alleged deconstruction of all ethical values, and many are left witnessing what they perceive to be nothing less than a free-for-all for moral superiority and domination. The story, as the media play it, is simultaneously "old and tired," yet still unfolding across America. How we work as a nation toward understanding what is really going on will very much determine the future of our democracy.

Perhaps this is why the issue of teaching values has become so contested, why people such as the Reverend Jerry Falwell and William Bennett ubiquitously appear on television, in print, and now online, waging their "noble crusade" to restore values in the United States. They speak passionately, if at times hypocritically, of family values, Christian (and begrudgingly Judeo) values, and of American values in general. Along with other religious and political leaders, they have been repeating these buzzwords of the political right for more than two decades. Today it seems as if everyone struggles to place herself or himself somewhere on the side of the good and the just, or at least not to be found standing alone on the wrong side of the issue. As a result, there has been a proliferation of editorials, news articles, and books announcing where people stand, and why they are standing there.

Not surprisingly, the right (as it has done so successfully with its "prolife" strategy) has unabashedly usurped "values" as it own concept and *raison d'être*. Conversely, the left has moved awkwardly, if not somewhat aimlessly, on this issue. Those who do speak out about values are vehemently accused by the right, and even by some within their own ranks, as merely undermining capitalists and Eurocentric values, the hallmarks of American life, while promoting cultural and moral relativism in the process. After all, so the argument goes, in the age of multiculturalism, how could anyone promote one value over another without being guilty of racism, sexism, or class elitism? Accordingly, anything that "privileges" one belief over another must be met with suspicion, if not rejected outright.

Paradoxically, we live at a time of heightened moral rhetoric and ever-growing intolerance of and violence toward those who are deemed deviant. Religious and political leaders in the United States as well as around the world keep exhorting us to adhere to the fundamentals of a moral life as they increasingly attack all who fall outside *their* vision of piety and justice. The lines are being drawn and the territory is being established; if outside the domain of the good, one is by definition an enemy of truth and justice. These days it is difficult to traverse even the shortest of distances without either trespassing on someone's moral property or insulting someone as one inadvertently moves on to another valued place. We apparently also live at a time when uncharted movement can cost us dearly.

The impact of all this on education can be readily observed at the various levels of instruction and policymaking. Arguments about how to teach or even acknowledge sexuality, race, multiculturalism, or ebonics, to name a just a few controversial subjects, dominate curriculum and local board meetings from New York to California. Such agenda items are among some of the more hotly debated topics, and all are being linked, one way or another, to the moral development of students. Thus urban, suburban, and rural educators all find themselves embroiled in the still-raging culture wars while they struggle to teach. *Teaching Values* is an attempt to analyze and discuss some of these education issues from a critical perspective. This volume, therefore, is not intended to be the last word about any of the topics discussed. Instead, the goal is to offer the reader a rigorous consideration or reconsideration of the issues and to promote similar atttempts at critical perspectives by others. In a sense, *Teaching Values* is intended as a kind of prolegomenon to any future investigation of connections to be made among education, politics, culture, and values.

This book is meant to provoke and to lay claim to the possibility that embracing values does not automatically make one dogmatic and intolerent—in other words, does not turn someone into a kind of religious fundamentalist or conservative extremist. But it also is a book designed to show just how often the claim to morality gets in the way of educating students, by confusing and promoting preferences for absolutes. The effort here is to offer the reader a book about some aspects of the struggle to come to terms with "teaching values," the values that educators employ in the name of teaching, and the teaching that educators advocate in the name of values.

For those looking for a simple or straightforward prescription of what is right and wrong in the classroom, this book will disappoint; indeed, it has an obligation to do so. Its purpose is not to offer anyone a guide to achieving moral certitude or even some helpful "tools" or "teaching aids" concerning moral character *per se*. To the contrary, *Teaching Values* is about reconsidering some of the many alleged moral principles at work in teaching, curriculum development, and educational policy. The critical perspectives in this volume are presented to the reader to assist in a process of reevaluation of the foundations and strategies we embrace in the name of teaching, something "good" teachers and all who are involved with education should do periodically.

In addition, it is hoped that this book will provide some useful discussion for those thinking about similar issues but not directly involved in the field of education. For too long, those claiming the moral authority to talk about values have monopolized the debate. *Teaching Values* is a gesture toward challenging that monopoly without attempting to replace it with yet another "totalizing" ready-made moral code or structure. The result is a series of discussions, analyses, and reflections that foster, as I suggest in the epilogue, the notion of teaching in an "extra-moral sense," a perspective I try to convey throughout the book.

Well before the "radical sixties" were identified as the watershed period of educational reform, the relationships among education, politics, culture, and values were explored and argued over by many who now form the pillars of the Western tradition, especially in the United States. From Plato to Milton to T. S. Eliot, the concern over politics, culture, values, and education has played an important role in the thinking and writing of just about every major or canonical figure of Western thought. So it is somewhat disconcerting that the desire by the left to continue exploring and analyzing the relationships among education, politics, culture, and values is considered by their conservative opponents as nothing more than necessary and pernicious outcomes of feminism, multiculturalism, postmodernism, and a host of other radical forms of "amoral" thinking. In short, the debate over teaching values has been too often hijacked and sent off course by the right, who appear intent on doing little else than turning the debate into an exclamation of lament over the legacy of the 1960s.

In my opinion, many on the left and those who identify themelves as postmodernists have either forfeited the issue of values to the right out of the fear of even sounding moralistic or have used methods and jargon that have so alienated even sympathetic audiences that the right has managed to take control of and dominate the debate about values in the Unitied States. Despite the fact that there has been much important and good work by those grouped under the rubric of postmoderism, the right has been able to take full advantage of the stylistic particularities and the often robotic methodology employed by some of those "deconstructing" this or that text or moral institution. The consequence of this has been devastating in a number of ways, but perhaps most importantly in the success the right has had in pulling the "values carpet" out from underneath the sometimes pretentious and often clumsy feet of many postmodern cultural critics.

What has made matters worse is the fact that many in the field of education have understandably and rightly turned to the language and logic of postmodernism in an effort to critically engage us with the important issues but too often wind up sounding like insecure academics trying to prove their philosophical dexterity and prowess. This has allowed the right to manipulatively place all postmodernists into the same cauldron of nihilistic obscurantism. Unfortunately this obfuscates the valuable work of Henry A. Giroux, bell hooks, Peter McLaren, Donaldo Macedo, and Cornel West, among others, who also make use of some of the same language and logic, and do so successfully in their own voice. It also has led to the wholesale rejection of the work of contemporary Continental thinkers such as Jacques Derrida and Michel Foucault by people who would benefit from knowing the work of these and other postmodern thinkers. Instead, people are offered caricatures of such writing and thinking and justifiably run away from the opacity and self-indulgence, but are nonetheless still missing out on something of value.

Teaching Values: Critical Perpectives on Education, Politics, and Culture is an attempt to pull the "values carpet" back out from under the right without falling prey to the pitfalls of such an endeavor, namely, of sounding (or being) as ideologically dogmatic about values as those on the right have proven to be or repeating the pseudo-postmodernist's mistake of confusing sarcasm and cynicism for irony. The critical perspectives offered here are an attempt to incorporate the sophistication and rigor that contemporary cultural criticism has developed over the years with a rather straightforward presentation of a few themes and issues that are worth our attention.

The book, as noted earlier, is a series of considerations and reconsiderations of topics I believe to be important for educators, and those interested in such issues, to discuss or revisit because of their complexity and significance. The critical perspectives on these topics are meant to offer the reader ways of approaching difficult and, to my mind, sometimes undervalued issues in a new light. The task of pursuing such an undertaking is admittedly daunting enough. There are, for example, so many issues to explore that omitting any will give rise to the suspicion of some unjustified bias. There are also many political traps to fall into, even if one proceeds with caution. Never-

theless, I believe that such a project is worth attempting because of the vacuum that has formed around the question of teaching values and the ensuing silence that now prevails among the left concerning this specific topic.

The motivation for writing this book comes from a variety of sources. In part, my experiences as director of the Graduate Program in Urban and Multicultural Education at the College of Mount Saint Vincent in the Bronx have convinced me of the need for such a book. Working with predominantly New York City teachers from many different neighborhoods throughout the five boroughs has resulted in my encountering emotions, ideas, and reactions to every educational, professional, and personal issue one could imagine. From a teacher coming to class after a stabbing to discussing community reaction to proposed changes in the curriculum to analyzing some educational policy blunder with people directly involved in the controversy or blacklash, I have had the chance to talk with teachers about the things that matter to them. The critical perspectives offered in this book are attempts to address some of the issues that have repeatedly emerged from the cacophony of complaints, frustrations, and confusion voiced by hardworking teachers in the program.

I have also had the opportunity and, in some cases, the privilege of working with people at every level of educational leadership in New York City and New York State, and feel strongly that the strategy and focus of this book are, in part, results of those interactions and collaborations. Throughout my tenure as an administrator of a rather unique program, I have been called upon to participate in and be a member of numerous committees and panels dealing with the professional development and preparation of teachers. Because of this work, I have encountered incredibly wonderful and dedicated people, all attempting to improve the profession of teaching. But I also have encountered the racism, class elitism, homophobia, and sexism that persist in the field of education and continue to work against the achievements of all teachers and students. *Teaching Values* is a response to all those remarks and questions that reveal the prejudice and ignorance that still guide much of the efforts to reform education. The critical perspectives offered here also attempt to say something after the hurt and shock of such encounters and to respond, as diplomatically as possible, to those who have said unjust things about students, teachers, parents, and just about anyone they could attack or blame for the failure of education and the decline of moral values in the United States.

To date there have been many books published about education, culture, and theory. Many of them are good books. Some attempt to contextualize current positions regarding philosophy of education, while others offer particular readings of a given subject, such as race, gender, or class; all of them make contributions to the field of education and cultural criticism. *Teaching Values* attempts to build on this body of work by combining my experiences of working with New York City school teachers, in and out of the classroom, the New York City Board of Education, and the United Federation of Teachers (the teachers union) with my own particular work on philosophy and culture. As in the case with many academics these days, it was my work in one field that led to a career in another. My study of contemporary Continental philosophy, focusing on race, class, and gender issues, led me to explore multiculturalism and education. *Teaching Values*, then, is a hybrid effort, as it were, a combination of my current work in the field of education and my continuing work in philosophy and culture.

This book is meant to be both modest and bold in its scope. It is modest to the degree that it simply offers some "critical perspectives" on the topics I consider of value. It does not presume to exhaust the issues discussed or to posit any absolute and final claims about the things under consideration. The book is bold, as I see it, to the degree that it reflects an honest struggle with the issues it does address and the manner in which they are discussed. By selecting the topics and themes presented in this book I have tried to highlight some of the values at play (and at work) in education today without explicitly laying out those values each and every time—sometimes I wanted the values in question to be identified or revealed through the working out of the given critical perspective. This is as much a methodological choice as it is a temperamental one, meaning it is my goal, in part, to suggest a way of working through these types of issues. As a result, some of the chapters read more personally than others, some more speculatively; however, I hope all read more persuasively than not.

Teaching Values consists of six explorations into some particular aspect of the relationships among education, politics, culture, and values. There is, in addition, an epilogue which is intended to discuss broadly the meaning and possibility of *teaching in an extra-moral sense*. In all the chapters I have tried my best to be true to my own spirit of inquiry and mindful of the likely audience of such a volume. I would like this book, among other things, to help forward the position that people influenced by postmodernism can offer something concrete and positive to the discussion about education, politics, culture, and values.

The first chapter, "When the Truth Is Gone: Teaching in an Age of Uncertainty," considers the issue of teaching in the age of postmodernism. This chapter discusses the implications of teaching after the loss of truth with a capital "T" and suggests, contrary to public opinion, that this particular age of uncertainty is not the result of the evils of postmodernists undermining the moral fabric of our knowledge system and our nation along with it, but is instead part of the very essence of the Western tradition so many are fighting to preserve.

"When the Truth Is Gone" acknowledges that there have been criticisms of and attacks on many of the hallmarks of Western culture, but it also suggests that calling into doubt previous "truths" is neither unique to postmodernism nor necessarily harmful to the ethical character of students. Rather than buy into the fears and charges raised by William Bennett, Dinesh D'Sousa, and others who have lamented the "devaluing of America," "When the Truth Is Gone" suggests that the force of postmodernism is consistent with the history of Western thought and perfectly aligned with American thinking, going back to Emerson.

The main thrust of "When the Truth Is Gone" is to note that this age of uncertainty is not the first age of uncertainty and is not one that leaves us without hope or love. Teaching during such a time, therefore, need not be understood as a time of loss, a time of longing for an earlier age of promise and values. Teachers and students may need to confront the fact that, as Michel Foucault puts it, "the task of telling the truth is an endless labor," but a labor that bears fruit. Teaching in an age of uncertainty need not be construed as teaching in an age of cynicism.

The second chapter, "Happy to Be Nappy," revisits the 1998 controversy involving Ruth Sherman, a white school teacher who unwittingly set off a political powder keg by teaching the children's book *Nappy Hair* to her third-grade class. This incident provides us with a great deal of material concerning the dynamics of teaching students of color in a racially charged context—that is, teaching just about anywhere in the United States today. By reconsidering the event, by examining, how the media presented and represented the incident, this chapter aims to expose some of the racism, sexism, and politics involved that distorted and discouraged any helpful dialogue concerning teaching and curriculum.

Instead of addressing the difficult issue of the dynamics

put into motion when teachers, especially white teachers, attempt to reach out to students of color by using "culturally relevant" materials, we were offered the moral and political outrage of all those who stood behind Ruth Sherman and her good intentions. No one, at the time, bothered to go beyond the immediate uproar and offer any serious consideration of the materials used, the teaching methods employed, and the issue of cross-cultural communication, namely, the establishing of trust.

"Happy to Be Nappy" is an attempt to identify some of the problems caused and ignored by media coverage of what became "the Ruth Sherman story." It also suggests an alternative direction of analysis that might have proven helpful in understanding why the parents of the community were so upset at the time with the use of the book *Nappy Hair*, and why the book may rightly be challenged. This chapter is not meant to answer all the lingering questions over this troubling moment in public education, but it does try to offer a critical overview to help explain what took place in the media, what issues need to be reexamined, what might be problematic with the book *Nappy Hair* and what other possible ways one could interrogate such a volatile issue. By looking into the eye of this educational and political storm, we can gain some insights into teaching all students and better preparing teachers to appropriately incorporate culturally relevant materials, especially for students of color.

The third chapter, "From Substandard to Nonstandard English: Getting beyond the Morality of Speaking Right," addresses the lingering notion that those who speak a nonstandard form of English are somehow engaging in a linguistically *sub*standard mode of expression and are thereby undermining the moral integrity of our democracy. This chapter discusses the presumption of the "superiority" of standard English over and above other forms of English, primarily

Black English or ebonics, and also looks at the relationships among language, politics, and power.

By analyzing some of the prevailing attitudes toward Black English, this chapter attempts to directly address the "morality of speaking right" maintained by many who are involved with teaching. The goal of this chapter is to make clear the distinction between the pragmatic benefits of speaking standard English to enhance and perpetuate our democracy and any meta- or nonlinguistic claims and attitudes about the moral status of standard and nonstandard forms of English. Arguing that people, but especially teachers, need to get beyond the limiting arrogance that artificially enhances the moral value of standard English by devaluing Black English, this chapter suggests that the rationale for embracing standard English need not rest on the trashing of Black English.

The history and politics of language in general, and in this case of standard English and Black English, is of genuine value to all who are working with students at every level of instruction. "From Substandard to Nonstandard English" attempts to get readers to more fully reconsider the history of Black English within the cultural, political, and historical context in which it developed. This chapter makes plain that the future of Black English and the ever-expanding standard English may well depend more upon nonlinguistic factors than many on both sides of the debate would like. "From Substandard to Nonstandard English" acknowledges that many in the field of teaching English and English as a Second Language have already recognized a lot, if not all, of this. The fact, however, that so many educators, administrators, and politicians continue to argue and function as if "the morality of speaking right" is still the heart of the matter, is the reason why this chapter offers one more attempt to expose the linguistic, pedagogical, and ethical flaws of such thinking.

The fourth chapter, "Go Tell It on the Mount," is intended

to give testimony to the importance of "place" and the mood of a place in education. This chapter offers the reader an assessment of the purpose and mission of the College of Mount Saint Vincent in relationship to developing a progressive graduate program in education and a successful collaboration with the New York City Teacher Center of the United Federation of Teachers. "Go Tell It on the Mount" describes the significance of a place such as the College of Mount Saint Vincent, a small liberal arts college founded by the Sisters of Charity, in the very large and image-conscious New York City. In a city where Columbia's Teachers College, Bank Street, and Fordham University dominate graduate programs in education, the College of Mount Saint Vincent has managed to make a genuine contribution toward the advancement of graduate education and the professional development of teachers in large measure due to the historic commitment of the Sisters of Charity to serving the diverse and underserved communities of New York City.

The mission of the Sisters of Charity led to the founding of the Graduate Program in Urban and Multicultural Education at the college. Once established, the program began to thrive because of the very nature of the sisters' commitment to social justice. The College of Mount Saint Vincent, guided by this mission, provided the perfect environment for a program dedicated to exploring and advancing urban education from a multicultural perspective. This chapter attempts to identify the spirit of place and the importance for those involved in education to be conscious of the significance of place in their daily practice. This chapter also presents the importance of other places, in this case specifically the New York City Teacher Center which is the Professional Development Program of the United Federation of Teachers. "Go Tell It on the Mount" attempts to describe the special relationship between two different places committed to serving teachers.

In the fifth chapter, "But Is He Straight? Identity, Teaching, and the Simple Acts of Privilege," readers are offered a discussion and analysis of how privilege works to produce the presumption of something like a simple act. By using Judith Butler's work on gender as a basis for criticism, "But Is He Straight?" attempts to have readers reconsider the nature and dynamics of classroom interactions once "simple acts" are called into question. Through using sexuality as a starting point, "But Is He Straight?" develops a critical perspective of the presumption of all simple acts emanating from within a context of privilege.

"But Is He Straight?" attempts to integrate Michel Foucault's thoughts on what he calls "techniques of the self" with the project of reconsidering one's own position of privilege (as teacher) within the classroom. By thinking through the issues of race, class, and gender as contributing factors to the "good" and "bad" interactions between teachers and students, the aim of this chapter is to consider ways of first acknowledging and then addressing the material reality of the simple acts of privilege in the classroom.

"But Is He Straight?" also offers a critical discussion about the very nature of "performing" acts (simple or otherwise) in the classroom. By introducing the reader to the novel perspective of the Brazilian theater director, theorist, and educator Augusto Boal, this chapter challenges educators to rethink our way of "acting" in the classroom. In addition to briefly discussing Boal's strategy for engaging with one another, this chapter refers to the work of Henry A. Giroux and bell hooks, among others, to offer one way toward reworking the presumption of the simple acts of privilege and moving beyond them in the name of critical pedagogy.

The sixth chapter, "Why Multiculturalism (*Still*)?," offers the reader a rationale for and a reconsideration of the continued role and importance of multicultural education. This chapter offers a challenge to Nathan Glazer's claim that multiculturalism is simply the "price" America is paying for failing to, in his words, "incorporate" African Americans into the mainstream. It goes on to offer an analysis of the arguments made against multiculturalism by the likes of Arthur Schlesinger Jr. and Diane Ravitch, who, like Glazer, are not right-wing fanatics and ought to be taken seriously. "Why Multiculturalism (*Still*)?" tries to show how Glazer, Schlesinger, and Ravitch nevertheless play into the hands of the extreme right and their concept of nationalism.

Using the work of James A. Banks to outline and discuss what he identifies as the five dimensions of multicultural education, "Why Multiculturalism (*Still*)?" presents the reader with the fundamental principles of multicultural education and how these dimensions are useful and important for teaching today. But the chapter also examines the "friendly confusion" over multiculturalism due to the work of philosophers and others who, in the name of multiculturalism, actually cause some problems.

"Why Multiculturalism (*Still*)?" also tries to show why multiculturalism is not to be confused with strategies that merely encourage "tolerating" others. Multiculturalism is instead presented in the context of attempting to foster social justice within the United States and not simply a means to gloss over the complexities and difficulties that are part of the reality of a nation of diverse peoples and cultures. Last, this chapter argues for the need to understand multiculturalism in terms of the prospect that there always will exist a gulf between those who dominate the political and cultural institutions of our nation (whoever they might be at any given time) and those who find themselves on the other side of the power structure.

The epilogue, "Teaching in an Extra-Moral Sense," offers the reader some reflections and positions concerning teaching in the context of understanding, promoting, and challenging values. This chapter is not intended to lay out a specific program for moral development or character education but rather presents a number of concerns and issues that are important to teaching values today, given the relationships among education, politics, and culture.

"Teaching in an Extra-Moral Sense" revisits Nietzsche's concern about the mandate for truthfulness understood as little more than the demand to lie according to fixed conventions. The epilogue then poses the question of what teaching would be like if such a mandate were confronted and shown to be the force behind unethical teaching and education. Teaching in an extra-moral sense would be teaching that would occur only after one were able to be free from the moral constraints that limit and harm us, that cause us to remain ignorant of the promise of values emerging from love and justice instead of prejudice and hate.

The epilogue explores some of the complicated, ambivalent, and ambiguous questions and situations that make up everyday life, and attempts to offer some thoughts about these issues in a practical manner. By examining some of the "moral" principles that allegedly guide teaching, this chapter will address the possibility of teaching in an extra-moral sense to foster a greater chance of working toward social justice in and out of schools. If teachers are going to be held in any way responsible for the moral character of their students, then teachers will need to confront their own ethical positions and be clear about the connections between their teaching and the values they are advocating or are being asked to promote.

Teaching Values: Critical Perspectives on Education, Politics, and Culture is a book intended to provoke further discussion about its content and the issue of values in education generally. Strictly speaking, this volume is not meant to definitively answer the right or even those on the left who believe that the "new philosophy" is morally bankrupt. Instead, *Teaching Values* aims at providing some provocative discussions, some critical perspectives, informed and influenced by postmoderism, that encourage more educators, and others interested as well, to pursue the issue of values and to begin to reclaim an ethical identity free from the dogma and mythology of the religious and political right. This book resists the all-or-nothing proposition wrongly posed by critics (and some advocates) of postmodernism and cultural theory regarding values and offers some perspectives that might lead to a renewed sense of teaching values.

It is in the spirit of continuing to identify and address issues that reveal, promote, and constrain values in education and beyond that this book is written. That we live during a time when many are still looking for quick and simple answers to difficult questions should not pursuade us to abandon this labor-intensive work. The many fast-mouthed moralists who urge us to join their ranks to decide right from wrong before it is too late must be reminded that the question of values is an old one, one that refuses to be answered quickly. *Teaching Values* is, in part, an appeal not to confuse moral impatience with ethical expedience. The critical perspectives offered here are attempts to keep the discussion going forward, but at a pace respectful of all those who have labored long and hard to make values matter.

1.

When the Truth Is Gone

Teaching in an Age of Uncertainty

And new Philosophy calls all in doubt,
The Element of fire is quite put out;
The Sun is lost, and th'earth, and no man's wit
Can well direct him where to look for it.
And freely men confesse that this world's spent,
When in the Planets, and the Firmament
They seeke so many new; then see that this
Is crumbled out againe to his Atomies.
'Tis all in pieces, all coherence gone;
All just supply, and all Relation:
Prince, Subject, Father, Son, are things forgot,
For every man alone thinkes he hath got
To be a Phoenix, and that then can bee
None of that kind, of which he is, but hee.
This is the Worlds condition now . . .

—John Donne, *An Anatomy of the World*

When the Truth is Found to be Lies,
And all the Joy Within You Dies.
Don't You Want Somebody to Love.
Don't You Need Somebody to Love.
Wouldn't You Love Somebody to Love.
You Better Find Somebody to Love.

—Jefferson Airplane, "Somebody to Love"

For the past twenty years or so, many Americans have worried out loud and complained about the loss of truth, with a capital "T," in our culture. Such concerns have come from all corners of the political landscape, but perhaps none as fervent or alarmist as those voiced by the religious and political right. Following the lead of the Reverend Jerry Falwell and Pat Robertson, conservative commentators and critics Dinesh D'Souza, Roger Kimball, Hilton Kramer, and William Bennett, have all voiced their outrage and frustration over the erosion of American values in general and education in particular. They claim, among other things, that this state of affairs is the direct result of contemporary America's rejection of the principles and tenets of the Enlightenment, the very foundation of our nation's way of life. The primary reason for this decay and loss of values is said to be due to "postmodernism" and the "tenured radicals," to use Kimball's term, who proselytize a cultural relativism, and consequent nihilism, to students across America, at every level of instruction. In the process, these postmodernists have been charged with undermining the very core of American education and the future of our democracy.

Summing up his position in his book *The De-Valuing of America: The Fight for Our Culture and Children*, William Bennett claims:

> [m]any of America's intellectual elite perpetrated a doctrine of *de facto* nihilism that cuts to the core of American traditions.... A lot of people forgot, and many others willfully rejected, the most basic and sensible answers to first questions, to questions about what contributes to our social well-being and prosperity, what makes for individual character and responsibility, and constitutes a "good society." (pp. 255–56)

According to Bennett and others, American educators, but especially humanities professors, have distracted students away from "the core of American traditions" and values with the skepticism and suspicion that, allegedly, comes with a postmodern perspective. Alluding to the work of the French philosopher Jacques Derrida, Bennett laments that "[s]ignificant portions of American society have been culturally deconstructed" (p. 256). The impact of this deconstruction, he claims, can be witnessed everywhere in American society: schools, universities, the legal profession, politics, and so on. For Bennett and other like-minded Americans, the task at hand is the "reconstruction" of America's cultural and moral values, and getting beyond the uncertainty of postmodernism.

But, as noted earlier, the right has not been alone in its criticism. Liberal and even "left progressives" also have expressed their concerns over the moral and political fallout of postmodernity. Author and democratic socialist Barbara Ehrenreich voiced her opinion on the matter at the 1991 Socialist Scholars Conference and subsequently published it in *Democratic Left*, a publication of the Democratic Socialists of America, as "The Challenge for the Left." She suggests that

> [a]t a deeper level though, any possibility of a moral perspective gets erased by a position fashionable among some of our post-modernist academics, that there can be no absolutes, no truths, and hence no grounds for moral judgments. There can't be a left if there's no basis for moral judgments, including judgments that will cut across group or gender or ethnic lines. (p. 337)

Fearing the loss of any moral authority to challenge corporate and capitalist interests, Ehrenreich exclaims her rejection of the "value-free" relativism supposedly espoused by postmodernist academics.

Progressives such as Ehrenreich who make such criticisms should not be misinterpreted as begin in a political alliance with the right, but they do indicate a shared fundamental distrust of the "consequences" of postmodernist thinking. Thus, the left as well as the right view postmodernists' inquiries into the historical and formal nature and function of concepts such as truth, reason, and rationality itself as under-cutting the possibility of moral action and the teaching of values. The presumption of those from both ends of the polit-ical spectrum is that whatever postmodernism has to offer, it cannot be good for America.

Enumerating his complaints concerning the impact of postmodernism on higher education, Dinesh D'Sousa warns us, in the last chapter of his bestselling *Illiberal Education: The Politics of Race and Sex on Campus*, that by the time a student graduates from an American college or university she or he will have been taught the following falsehoods:

> that justice is simply the will of the stronger party; that standards and values are arbitrary, and the ideal of the educated person is largely a figment of bourgeois white male ideology, which should be cast aside; that individual rights are a red flag signaling social privilege, and should be subordinated to the claims of group interest; that all knowledge can be reduced to politics and should be pursued not for its own sake but for the political end of power; that convenient myths and benign lies can substi-tute for truth; that double standards are acceptable as long as they are enforced to the benefit of minority victims; that debates are best conducted not by rational and civil exchange of ideas, but by accusation, intimida-tion, and official prosecution; that the university stands for nothing in particular and has no claim to be exempt from outside pressures; and that the multiracial society cannot be based on fair rules that apply to every person, but must rather be constructed through a forced rationing of power among separatist racial groups. In

short, instead of liberal education, what American students are getting is its diametrical opposite, an education in closed-mindedness and intolerance, which is to say, illiberal education. (p. 229)

With this list of consequences, is it any wonder that postmodernism finds itself the anathema for all those committed to "properly" educating America? The perversion of education, then, as denoted by D'Sousa, stems from the loss of truth and reason, and their being replaced, according to him, by the cynical manipulation of emotion and the uncivil desire for power. This is the view of postmoderism that has so many demanding a return to a values-centered education, a return to objectivity, to truth and beauty. Of course, D'Sousa et al. never seem too bothered by any of the historical events or circumstances that might cause one to interpret things differently.

Expressing his assessment of the situation at the same Socialist Scholars Conference as Ehrenreich in 1991 and subsequently published as "Diverse New World" in the same edition of *Democratic Left* in the July/August 1991 volume, then Harvard professor of African American studies and philosophy of religion Cornel West challenges the views of D'Sousa. West points out that

> [w]e're not naive, we know that argument and critical exchange are not the major means by which social change takes place in the world. But we recognize that it has to have a role, has to have a function. Therefore, we will trash older notions of objectivity, and not act as if one group or community or one nation has a god's eye view of the world. Instead we will utilize forms of intersubjectivity that facilitate critical exchange even as we recognize that none of us are free of presuppositions and prejudgments. We will put our arguments on the table

and allow them to be interrogated and contested. The
quest for knowledge without presuppositions, the quest
for certainty, the quest for dogmatism and orthodoxy and
rigidity is over. (pp. 331–32)

West directly confronts D'Sousa by boldly stating that "we
will trash older notions of objectivity" and by proclaiming that
the quest for certainty, dogmatism, orthodoxy, and rigidity is
over. But far from trashing argument and critical exchange,
West acknowledges the need for intellectual and political
dialogue. In addition, he also asserts the need for the utiliza-
tion of various forms of "intersubjectivity," that is to say,
different voices and perspectives, which in turn can facilitate
the very critical, and civil, exchange sought by D'Sousa. The
postmodernist's rejection of truth with a capital "T," then, is
not so much a rejection of intellectual rigor, inquiry, and
values as much as a refusal to acquiesce in the prevailing
dogma that has in fact excluded many from full participation
in the search for meaning and value.

That this position strikes some as politically dangerous to
the security of the status quo is fair enough, but to condenm
this view as undermining American education and rendering
students closed-minded and intolerant ignores the political
and intellectual history that such a view challenges. What
D' Sousa and Bennett state as their fear, a political ideology
indifferent to truth and values, masks their desire to preserve
the political regime challenged by postmodernists, a challenge
that *does not* throw "truth" out the window. As Michel
Foucault, one of postmodernism's icons, points out in an interview with François Ewald, subsequently titled "The Concern
for Truth" for the French journal, *Magazine littéraire 207*;

[n]othing is more inconsistent than a political regime
that is indifferent to truth; but nothing is more danger-

ous than a political system that claims to lay down the truth. The function of "telling the truth" must not take the form of law, just as it would be pointless to believe that it resides by right in the spontaneous interplay of communication. The task of telling the truth is an endless labor: to respect it in all its complexity is an obligation which no power can do without—except by imposing the silence of slavery. (p. 267)

The challenge that many postmodernists have made is the challenge of honoring the very obligation that Foucault speaks of, that of respecting truth *in all its complexity*. It is perhaps the rendering complex what was previously accepted as "the simple truth" that so disturbs and frightens those who believe postmodernism is sounding the death knell for values.

Clearly we live during an age in which "new Philosophy calls all in doubt" and this has caused disruptions and disconti- nuities. Unfortunately, the resulting challenges to the hege- mony of Eurocentrism and phalocentrism voiced by feminists and antiracists, among others, have caused a blacklash, a nostalgic longing for the truth of things. With respect to education, this blacklash has been expressed by those demand- ing a cultural literacy that articulates the truth and values of our culture. As E. D. Hirsch Jr. puts it in his much-celebrated book, *Cultural Literacy: What Every American Needs to Know*:

> [t]o thrive, a child needs to learn the traditions of the particular human society and culture it is born into. Like children everywhere, American children need traditional information at a very early age. (p. 31)

This is the view that D'Sousa, Bennett, et al. offer as the only viable alternative to the destructive forces of postmodernism, which, they assert, continue to erode our belief in American traditions and values. Of course, Hirsch, now famous for his essential list of names, phrases, dates, and concepts, argues for a "cultural literacy" based on the traditional information one needs to know in order to succeed in the United States—indeed, what the United States needs to succeed, that is, to survive.

Hirsch prophesizes that

> [w]e will be able to achieve a just and prosperous society only when our schools ensure that everyone commands enough shared background knowledge to be able to communicate effectively with everyone else. (p. 32)

Accordingly, unless we learn a shared history, we will not be able to effectively communicate with each other and do the work necessary to ensure the future of our democracy. Postmodernists are charged with threatening this noble project by trashing the validity of the traditions that would make up our "shared background knowledge" and by imposing all sorts of new, culturally relative, values.

The question here is not whether a "shared background knowledge" is important to the workings of our democracy; of course such knowledge is valuable. We need, however, to examine what gets considered to be part of this "shared" knowledge, what gets included and excluded, and by whom. What Hirsch and the hundreds of thousands of parents and teachers who bought his book (primarily for the "list") never ask are the following questions: Who gets to determine the "shared" knowledge? Who gets to compose the list? And further, What general (read "national") meaning can such a list have?

Barbara Herrnstein Smith argues in her essay "Cult-Lit: Hirsch, Literacy, and the National Culture" that

> [t]he method by which the List was generated is, in any case, exceedingly mysterious. According to Hirsch, it is

not "a complete catalogue of American knowledge," but "is intended to illustrate the character and range of the knowledge literate Americans tend to share" and to "establish guideposts that can be of practical use to teachers, students, and all others who need to know our literate culture" (which is, of course, according to Hirsch, "every American"). But one might ask (granting the double absurdity of a specifically "American knowledge" and a possible catalog of *any* actual human knowledge), what sorts of persons are the "literate Americans" whose knowledge is illustrated or represented by the List? How, for example, could one distinguish them from Americans who merely know how to read? And how does Hirsch himself know what "the literate reader" knows? (p. 86)

The questions asked by Smith should be cause for concern to everyone interested in helping establish a "shared" knowledge base. Beyond the obvious, Smith alludes to the problems of attempting to articulate an "American knowledge." The reasons for the problems are complex, but one thing is for certain: Many Americans are ignorant of their shared history, though they are quite literate.

Donaldo Macedo bravely challenges the ignorance of Americans in his *Literacies of Power: What Americans Are Not Allowed to Know* and those institutions that are responsible for producing and maintaining this sad condition. Macedo discusses how various institutions, but

particularly schools, reproduce the dominant ideology through a web of lies that distort and transfigure reality. Central to this cultural reproductive mechanism is the overcelebration of myths that inculcate us with beliefs about the supremacy of Western heritage at the same

time as the dominant ideology creates other instruments
that degrade and devalue other cultural narratives along
the lines of race, ethnicity, language, and gender. (p. 37)

What Macedo denounces is the selectivity of information
typically presented to students about the nation they live in as
well as the world as a whole, a selectivity that Hirsch would
argue is based on truth and merit. Macedo's criticism rightly
rejects the premise of the "selective view" and demands the
debunking of the myths sustained by schools across America,
the myths that "overcelebrate" Columbus, the Pilgrims, and
westward expansion and that downplay, if not outright
exclude, the history of slavery, the genocide of Native Americans, the role of women and people of color in building our
democracy, how the United States came to "gain" Puerto Rico
as a territory, and so on.

The stance against the myths and lies taken by Macedo
and others provokes the ire of those "traditionalists" who see
such criticism as attacks on the very soul of our nation. The
traditionalists view the reevaluation of American history by
postmodernist academics (liberal elites, according to Bennett)
such as Macedo as little more than a process in which the
truth gets replaced with lies. "Too often," according to
Bennett,

the American people have deferred to the views of the
elite on these matters. When they have done so, they
have for the most part hurt themselves, their interests,
their beliefs, and most important, their children. When
they have heeded the elites, things have gotten worse—
sometimes a lot worse. (p. 38)

To get out of harm's way, Bennett insists upon the return to
the institutions and values that made us a great nation in the

first place, a return to the myths that Macedo begs us to move beyond. This is the struggle.

No one involved with the struggle to respect telling the truth "in all of its complexity" denies the significance of myths and stories to help promote a general sense of common or shared "knowledge," especially for young children. But the position taken by the traditionalists, that listening to postmodernist academics will only lead to harm, distorts the criticism of the selectivity of the myths that are being challenged. Today the study of the "discovery" of America may be less full of the images of a Columbus fulfilling a divine mission, but is, nevertheless, still promoting a mythology of the birth of our nation without telling the truth in all of its complexity.

Herbert Kohl offers a perfect example of the continuation of turning a blind eye toward the teaching of history in his essay "Uncommon Differences: On Political Correctness, Core Curriculum, and Democracy in Education." Kohl examines a relatively contemporary history textbook used in many schools. He notes that

> [t]he Addison-Wesley high school textbook *United States History from 1865*, volume 2 (1986) summarizes U.S. history from "prehistory to 1850" in pages 4 to 31. African-American peoples enter the stage of U.S. history on page 8 in the following words: "Traders also exchanged New England rum in Africa for slaves to be sold in the West Indies or the Thirteen Colonies." Aside from the historical falsity of the assertion that rum was the sole medium of exchange in the slave trade and its racist implications for current debates on substance abuse, there is the question of people being introduced as slaves. Were they slaves or were they carpenters, kings, weavers, farmers, etc, who were stolen into slavery? Whose perspective do we want our children to take? (pp. 109–110)

As Kohl argues, such a description (myth?) "destroys black people's identity by starting from slavery rather than from Africa prior to slavery" (p. 110). Such a narrative provides little that could be understood as positive, and nothing from a perspective other than the slave traders and owners. It suggests that Africans, as slaves, could not offer anything of value other than their involuntary labor. With such a narrative we end up with a not-so-subtle tautology: Africans were slaves, slaves have little, if anything to offer the New World other than their enslavement, thus their status as slaves. There is nothing prior, no other narrative to fill out the much more rich and complex history of the people being described (created).

Kohl rightly notes that

> [i]t is personhood, culture, and humanity that Afrocentric and other ethnocentric curricula try to provide, as well as more historical truth than is allowed in our history textbooks. There are unpleasant aspects of our national history, and it is better for our children to know about them than to become party to reproducing them. (p. 110–111)

Even if one disagrees with introducing children to those aspects of our history and culture that Kohl generously identifies as "unpleasant," it is hard to argue against the desire to eliminate the distorted, simplistic, and therefore false images produced and reproduced by such descriptions, perspectives, and beliefs. Bennett would counter that

> this does not mean we have to stop teaching history, stop teaching what we know to be true, stop teaching the difference between right and wrong. . . . (p. 218)

There is no doubt that one could find support for the narrative that Kohl criticizes—that is, one could present some selective evidence and ignore much else that would complicate things. But would this leave us with "what we know to be true"? Kohl and other progressive educators (among them Giroux, Macedo, and McLaren) have argued for years to do precisely what Bennett wants to do, namely "teach the difference between right and wrong" and "what we know to be true." But as all of these "critical pedagogues" have argued, such teaching is complex and demands teaching different truths—that is to say, demands, as Foucault put it, respecting the task of telling the truth "in all of its complexities."

Teaching these days, then, is necessarily teaching in an age of uncertainty. This is so, not because there is no truth to be discovered, but because of the desire to respect the truth (whatever that may turn out to be). It is an age of uncertainty because of the challenges to the "truths" that have reigned so long, and because more of the truth is being told. Many of those on the right demanding a return to truth and values would have us believe that the project of critical evaluation and exploration of the texts and strategies used to teach is somehow un-American, unpatriotic in the act of "deconstructing" our cultural institutions and principles. But clearly this is not the intent of such dedicated teachers struggling to be rigorous and thorough, struggling to gain new ground. Such a criticism also ignores the very American tradition of reconsidering the nature of things and the status of those things held to be dear and true.

In his introduction to "Nature," Ralph Waldo Emerson asks

> Why should not we also enjoy an original relation to the universe? Why should not we have a poetry and philosophy of insight and not of tradition, and a religion by revelation to us, and not the history of theirs? Embosomed for a season in nature, whose floods of life stream

around and through us, and invite us, by the powers they supply, to action proportioned to nature, why should we grope among the dry bones of the past, or put the living generation into masquerade out of its faded wardrobe? The sun shines to-day also. There is more wool and flax in the fields. There are new lands, new men, new thoughts. Let us demand our own works and laws and worship. (p. 7)

Emerson, certainly not a postmodernist, calls for an all-out intellectual, aesthetic, and spiritual revolution. His demand for an original relation to the universe is "the American cultural" call to arms. It is hardly the case that Emerson rejected, out of hand, all that was good, true, and beautiful, but his exhortation is a plea for new perspectives, new thoughts, new laws, new worship. How is Emerson's American manifesto different from Cornel West's claim that "we will trash older notions of objectivity"?

In some real sense Cornel West is the heir to a distinctly American tradition, a tradition of a philosophical thinking called pragmatism, a tradition that established "new rules" for truth. One could argue that far from undermining "American values," West is an example of embodying American truth and value. By posing challenges to truth "as given," West is in step with the pragmatists' program set in motion by Charles S. Peirce, William James, and John Dewey. All of these valued American thinkers had strong, and to some emboldened, notions about truth. One characteristically bold statement by William James can be found in his essay "Pragmatism's Conception of Truth." In this essay James asserts the following:

Truth lives, in fact, for the most part on a credit system. Our thoughts and beliefs "pass," so long as nothing challenges them, just as banknotes pass so long as nobody refuses them. But this all points to direct face-to-face verifications somewhere, without which the fabric of truth collapses like a financial system with no cash-basis whatever. You accept my verification of one thing, I yours of another. We trade on each other's truth. But beliefs verified concretely by *somebody* are the posts of the whole superstructure. (p. 433)

This is not to suggest that West and others pigeonholed into the category of postmodernity are committed to the "same" program as the pragmatists (there are significant differences among the pragmatists themselves). It does, however, indicate that there is an established American tradition of daring to ask difficult questions that take issue with the prevailing notions of truth, value, and certainty, a tradition that goes back at least to Emerson and one finding expression today in a variety of academic disciplines.

Articulating this view specifically within the context of postmodern education in his book *Critical Pedagogy and Predatory Culture: Oppositional Politics in a Postmodern Era*, Peter McLaren straightforwardly asks the following difficult questions:

Dare we conspire to create a critical pedagogy that is able to provide conditions for students to reject what they experience as a given; a pedagogy that includes a sharpened focus on the relationship among economies of capital investment, political economies, moral economies, economies of "free" expression, sexual economies, economies of belief and identity formation and the construction of desire and formation of human will; a pedagogy of discontent and of outrage that is able to contest the hegemony of prevailing definitions of the everyday as the "way things are"; a pedagogy that refuses the hidebound distinction between lofty expression and popular culture, between art and experience, between reason and imagination? We need a critical pedagogy in our colleges of education that can problematize schooling as a site for the construction of moral, cultural, and national identity, and emphasize the creation of the schooled citizen as a form of emplacement, as a geopolitical construction, as a process in the formation of the geography of cultural desire. Dare we transform teaching practices in our schools into acts of dissonance and interventions into the ritual inscription of our students into codes of the dominant culture; into structured refusals to naturalize existing relations of power; into the creation of subaltern counterpublics? (p. 21)

Certainly such a series of questions raised in such a passionate tone is partly the reason the religious and political right is so defensive about who is teaching these days and about who is asking questions. But even an antagonistic reader will spot McLaren's clear desire for social justice, moral integrity, and national identity, the very things that D'Sousa, Bennett, et al. are ostensibly trying to "reconstruct." The difference, however, is that McLaren is predicating such desire upon a democratic impulse, one that challenges the status quo and attempts to solicit greater participation from all Americans. McLaren's "daring" questions are in keeping with those who have "dared" to ask about the status of things before them. In so questioning, from a "postmodern" perspective, McLaren and others are exhibiting a peculiar American trait traceable all the way back to the very un-postmodern "transcendentalist" Emerson.

Of course, the desire to question is not exclusively an American impulse, although I have been attempting to suggest that there is a particular American tradition of such questioning and that "American postmodernists" are in fact part of that tradition, not outside of it. But it is important to remember that many others outside the United States who struggle with challenging oppressive and stultifying pedagogies and who have influenced progressive American educators have been dealing with such issues for years as well. The act of questioning itself is the subject of much discussion and is an issue dear to all who resist the models of education that discourage or ignore the liberating power of questioning.

In their evocative dialogue on education, published under the title *Learning to Question: A Pedagogy of Liberation*, Antonio Faundez notes to Paulo Freire that

> [i]n teaching, questions have been forgotten. Teachers and students alike have forgotten them, and, as I understand it, all knowledge begins from asking questions. It begins with what you, Paulo, call curiosity. But curiosity is asking questions! (pp. 34–35)

Curiosity is asking questions, but asking questions can prove painful and disruptive, as such "questioning" is often met with resistance and hostility. Many postmodernists have been accused of asking harsh and mean-spirited questions just for the sake of disrupting the order of things. I suppose that there are those who act in such a manner, but this can hardly be the rationale for dismissing the challenges that postmoderism and its diverse advocates pose to the current state of education, from elementary school through graduate education.

It is worth noting that Socrates, one of the pillars of Western culture and thought, and one seen as an exemplar of virtue by Bennett et al., also was accused of corrupting youth with his "method" of questioning. In the dialogue "Euthyphro," Plato has Socrates respond to Euthyphro's question of why Socrates is being prosecuted by Meletus:

What for? Not on trivial grounds, I think. It is no small thing for so young a man to have formed an opinion on such an important matter. For he, he says, knows how the young are corrupted, and who are their corrupters. He must be a wise man who, observing my ignorance, is going to accuse me to the state, as his mother, of corrupting his friends. . . .

The Athenians, it seems to me, may think a man to be clever without paying him much attention, so long as they do not think that he teaches his wisdom to others. But as soon as they think that he makes other people clever, they get angry, whether it be from resentment, as you say, or for some other reason. (pp. 1–2)

Plato portrays Socrates' philosophical method throughout the dialogues as an unrelenting questioning of the given dogma of the day, and without concern for the personal pain that might result from it. Asking questions and calling things into doubt eventually led to Socrates' death. As noted Plato scholar and translator F. M. Cornford observed in his book *Before and after Socrates*:

It is not surprising that the elder citizens of Athens, when they learnt (perhaps from disagreeable encounters with their own adolescent sons) that Socrates encouraged the young to call in question every moral precept, . . . concluded that he was demoralizing the young men. (p. 47–48)

The antagonism toward and fear of those who "question" have a long (and violent) history. That those asking questions today and rejecting the "givens" of our cultural history are seen as pariahs and are under attack should also not be "surprising." After all, such questioning does cause pain and discomfort, and demands the reconsideration of many people, concepts, and values that have long enjoyed the status of being "good" for every American. It seems, therefore, easy to simply assert that the blame for what's wrong today is due to those individuals calling all into doubt.

It is understandable why people resist, as many have done and no doubt will continue to do, when confronted by difficult challenges that can disrupt our lives. Such challenges can prove to be discomforting and even painful. If the world is not as we thought it to be, it's hard to know who or what to trust. But too often, people confuse what is unpleasant and painful with what causes us harm. In doing so, they are quick to dismiss or discredit (and sometimes destroy) those who are perceived as causing the harm.

This has been the reaction to many of the cultural, political, and intellectual transformations that have occurred in the United States since its beginning. In more recent times the struggle to reconsider the status and value of African Americans, women, Native Americans, Hispanics, lesbians, and gays, and of many others who have challenged the "given truths" about their histories and identities, is viewed as an attack on all that is good in the United States. The attempts by the religious and political right to "conserve" those truths that maintain the life they value must come, necessarily, at the expense of those asking questions. For with such questions comes the need to reconsider and reevaluate, and therefore to live in an age of uncertainty. But this need not mean living in an age without meaning and value. Teaching during such a time demands courage, integrity, and love. The task of such teaching, of "teaching to transgress," as bell hooks, following Paulo Friere's lead, understands it, is to engage in education as the practice of freedom.

The desire for such freedom, for liberation from the constraints of the various modes of prejudice and oppression that have and continue to work their way through our society and schools, is not an immoral desire, not an unpatriotic desire, but an instinctive desire to move on, a desire in the tradition of American political and intellectual history. That there are some who might exploit such a desire to "undo" everything that matters, out of anger and confusion, should not undermine the ethical thrust of such a desire, of such a movement. Teaching in *this* age of uncertainty is teaching in an age of transgression, of possibility. But then genuine teaching is always about questioning, challenging, transgressing, and new positions.

Certainly, thinkers and critics identified as postmodernists have called many things into doubt; thus the fear of those who wonder where all the questioning will ultimately leave us. For some reason the right presumes that it alone can guide the moral direction of our nation and do so prescriptively. Americans are made to fear the downfall of all that is good by those who dare question "the given truths" about the way we live. By calling into question racism, sexism, homophobia, class elitism, and other boundaries that hinder, if not, prevent democratic interaction and progress, we stray too far from the the truth according to the right. We are ordered to return from our transgressions, to come back to "family values," to the time-honored beliefs and practices of the Judeo-Christian tradition, and we are even given a "list" of the things that matter to any literate person living in the United States today. To do otherwise, to teach otherwise, is to be party to the "deconstruction" of our cultural institutions.

But an educated democratic society must consider and reconsider "the truths" upon which its culture is founded in order to live those truths that do hold up to such evaluation, and be prepared to move beyond those that do not. We must therefore teach to transgress—that is, teach to confront those things that have been merely imposed as true, and teach so that we can move beyond such truth, through the ambiguity and uncertainty that such transgression, such exploration demands. As Parker J. Palmer notes in his book *The Courage to Teach*,

> [w]hen my students and I discover uncharted territory to explore, when the pathway out of a thicket opens up before us, when our experience is illumined by the lightning-life of the mind—then teaching is the finest work I know. (p. 1)

Teaching is about seeking that uncharted territory to explore. Yet, such exploration is not without risk and failure; sometimes teachers and students do not get very far at all, never find the pathway out of a thicket; sometimes we all get lost. The point, however, is pushing on, regardless of the uncertainty of the journey, regardless if the truth is gone.

When the truth is gone, new truths may arise, not out of a vacuum but from within the very history in which they were hidden and kept secret. Those teachers committed to teaching in an age of uncertainty are committed to pursuing the truths that got left behind, forgotten, untold, and undiscovered. That some of these new truths may disrupt the comfort of those who have enjoyed the truth of things as they have been given should not thwart those committed to "telling the truth in all of its complexity." When the truth is gone, it is the love, courage, and integrity of those who teach that shine and are certain. Those who have attempted to portray the people asking questions as "the threat from within" have wrongly identified the threat to our nation's well-being.

Teaching in this age of uncertainty is teaching to restore the joy that learning the truth in all its complexity can bring. It is teaching the truths about things we have been given and asking questions that matter, questions that are asked out of defiance and out of love. Teachers across America working with students who have discovered that the "given truth" is found to be lies, or at least inconsistent with their everyday lived experience and the joy within them dies, as has been discussed by Jonathan Kozol, Cornel West, bell hooks, and others, are working to restore hope. When the truth is gone, it is the strength and love of those asking questions that offer our nation a chance to continue its progress toward justice.

2.

Happy to Be Nappy

In late November 1998, many New Yorkers found themselves animated, divided, troubled, and confused by the news coverage of a young white teacher named Ruth Sherman and a children's book entitled *Nappy Hair*. The book, written by African-American author and scholar Carolivia Herron, is the story of a young girl's successful struggle with other people's problems about and with her "nappy" hair. By using the book in her third-grade class at P.S. 75 in the Bushwick section of Brooklyn, Sherman had unwittingly set off a cultural and political powder keg in that predominantly Hispanic and African American community. The resulting explosion caused repercussions still needing to be more fully discussed and analyzed.

During a special morning meeting on Monday, November 23, with the school's principal, Felicita Santiago, a group of outraged parents accused Sherman of being racially insensitive at best, if not outright racist, by choosing to read *Nappy Hair* to her class. At some point during the meeting with the parents, Santiago summoned Sherman from the class she was teaching to come join them in the auditorium. The exchange quickly got heated, and Sherman was verbally attacked by those who came to the meeting armed with "proof" that the book she was teaching was offensive. Apparently a few of the angry group of parents had, in hand, black-and-white photocopies of pictures from the book, along with sections of the narrative, and distributed them to others in attendance. Eventually threats were voiced concerning Sherman's safety, and after a woman made what appeared to be a menacing gesture toward Sherman, Principal Santiago and a school security guard whisked her away from the crowd. The following day, Ruth Sherman was removed from her classroom responsibilities at P.S. 75 and sent to the office of her superintendent, Felix Vazquez, in School District 32 to perform nonteaching duties. Within days of the confrontation and her removal from school, Sherman publicly declared her inability to ever return to P.S. 75, claiming "I feel so badly for the kids, but I can't live like this—always looking over my shoulder.... I don't feel safe there" (*New York Post*, December 1, 1998).

The story of Ruth Sherman is a particularly difficult one to analyze, in part because of the superficial simplicity of the incident that led the media, and in turn many of those following the story, in the wrong direction. But it is also due to the profound problem of racism and sexism at work behind the news story of an earnest, young, first-year teacher being misunderstood and rejected by parents, most of whom, by the way, neither read the entire book nor had children in Ruth Sherman's class—only one of the fifty or so parents in attendance at the meeting that day had a child in Sherman's class. The difficulties of this story are worth wading through, however, because they offer insight into the complexities of teaching in a racially charged context and highlight a real problem of cross-cultural interactions—namely, trust.

One reason why the story of Ruth Sherman should be of importance to anyone involved with or interested in the practice of teaching urban students of color is the way the story so quickly became the saga of Ruth Sherman. Sherman was instantly embraced by the news media as the victim of ill-informed, hostile, and unappreciative parents, the victim of indifferent administrators, and the victim of a climate influenced by political correctness and the knee-jerk rejection of white benevolence. As *New York Post* columnist Andrea Peyser states it:

> In a world rapidly turning into a politically correct police state, an idealistic young teacher named Ruth Sherman has been tried, convicted and sentenced to threats of death for attempting to instill pride in impoverished Brooklyn students.
>
> Or, more specifically, the unwritten statute under which Sherman has been found guilty might be called: Teaching Equality While White. (*New York Post*, December 1, 1998, p. 7)

The speed with which so many came to embrace this perspective made it virtually impossible, at the time, for a more thoughtful and rigorous discussion to take place about Sherman's teaching, the book *Nappy Hair* itself, and the complicated issue of cross-cultural dynamics.

It is not the case that there is no truth to what Peyser reports as the story, namely that there exists a politically charged context in which all teachers work and that race often further defines that context. It should be noted, however, that the public debate over the matter, such as it was, went in one direction only, following guideposts that pointed a well-trodden way while ignoring other, more difficult, paths of consideration. The result was as predictable as it was wrong; everyone lost their way by myopically tracking what happened to Ruth Sherman and never dared venture beyond that boundary. But if one is willing to do even a bit of wandering, other aspects to this drama unfold, bringing us closer perhaps to the very precipice that the Ruth Sherman story attempted to keep us from seeing.

As the Nobel laureate novelist Toni Morrison acutely notes in her introduction to *Race-ing, Justice, En-gendering Power*, "in virtually all of this nation's great debates, nonwhites and women figure powerfully, although their presence may be disguised, denied, or obliterated" (p. xix). I want to suggest that the Ruth Sherman story is one more example of this phenomenon, and a moment of possible educative progress and public insight was lost in the process. The reasons for all this may prove to be complicated but they are identifiable. To ignore what and who got disguised, denied, or obliterated is to relegate this painful and awkward incident to a realm of confusion maintained by the racism and sexism that controlled this story from the start. I am convinced, however, that a careful analysis will reveal some twists and turns worth noting and might prove of some value for future attempts at cross-cultural interaction in and out of the classroom.

There are to my mind particular aspects of this story that need to be highlighted and critically discussed to get beyond the story as it was told. It is important, for example, to look at how Ruth Sherman was made the victim of this story; how the merits of the book *Nappy Hair* as a narrative promoting self-esteem were not sufficiently discussed; how the parents of the school were portrayed as the real culprits of this story; and how the "culture wars" (read "political correctness") were identified, yet again, as the cause for an overreaction—in this case, by people of color too eager for a fight. Each of these provides fertile ground for discussion and positive movement.

Perhaps the most striking feature of the Ruth Sherman story is precisely the fact that she became the heart and soul of the story for the mainstream media and how quickly all eyes turned toward her as the only legitimate victim. Bizarrely enough, Sherman was, to paraphrase Toni Morrison, disguised, denied, and obliterated in the process of being identified as a victim, and this dimension of the story failed to get any attention at the time.

When all was said and done, Sherman became the cute poster girl for white intervention, the well-intentioned do-gooder vilified by the very community she served. It was this double-edged sword that cut its way through the body of the story. It remains this double-edged sword of racism and sexism that works to distort a painful pedagogical moment and assigns blame. We must drop this sword to gain a better understanding of what took place.

As already noted, Ruth Sherman was identified as the victim. Although the *New York Post*'s reporting offers the best and most straightforward example, the *Post* was certainly not alone in this portrayal. *Newsweek*'s coverage by Lynette Clemetson further distorted the story in a number of significant ways. In its December 14, 1998, issue, *Newsweek* managed to present Ruth Sherman as a "national affairs" story, not as an education item. This editoral choice alone gives some indication of the path *Newsweek* decided to take. But if further clarification were necessary, *Newsweek* made sure all who read the story knew exactly why this was a national affairs story. The subheading to the section simply read: "Culture Wars." This along with the provocative story title, "Caught in the Cross-Fire: A young star teacher finds herself in a losing racial battle with parents," guaranteed that the story was to be considered part of the national culture wars debate and part of the movement to debunk political correctness.

The narrative and visual imagery of Ruth Sherman presented by *Newsweek* gives us, perhaps unintentionally, a contradictory figure—namely, Ruth Sherman, victim and vixen. The official story was reported in the same emotionally charged and laden writing as it was in the *Post*. This time, however, the representation of Ruth Sherman was morphed from the innocent, teary-eyed novice into the self-assured, glamorous woman teacher who nevertheless remains the victim of the hysteria created by parents driven by unbridled racial prejudice and dogmatic adherence to the tenets of political correctness. The *Newsweek* story, like the *Post's* depiction, then, is really a complex of stories: a tale of political correctness gone crazy, the portrait of a woman "caught in the cross-fire," as the article is titled, and the implication that blacks have self-esteem issues so problematic that they are torn among themselves as to how to educate their children.

To appreciate fully the transformation of Ruth Sherman from the *Post's* teary-eyed frightened novice to *Newsweek's* self-confident star teacher, we have to pay attention to both the language and the images used to present Sherman to readers. In doing so, we will see how sexism was actually deployed in the name of this woman. The front page of the *Post* had a photograph of Sherman looking nervously off into the distance with the headline "Tears for Teacher." Set within the black-and-white photograph is one sentence simply stating, "Teacher Ruth Sherman taunted by parents for using the black-pride book *Nappy Hair* in class, won't return to the school because she fears for her life." Below the headline we are told that it is her students who are crying for their "terrorized instructor."

The front page, of course, doesn't tell the whole story, but it does in fact tell the story that the *Post* wants its readers to have. In a dramatic and sensationalized delivery we have the image of a frightened young white woman along with the information that she was taunted and now fears for her life. Inside the paper we further find out that a group of "community activists" instigated the entire controversy, prompting *Post* columnist Peyser to wonder:

> How can a system that protects the likes of a Leonard Jeffries—the City College professor who uses his taxpayer-paid platform to preach anti-Semitism—turn its back on a white teacher who was motivated by nothing more sinister than a profound belief that black is beautiful? (*New York Post*, December 1, 1998, p. 7)

We quickly and erroneously move from an example of cross-cultural confusion to systemic corruption and a perversion of intentions. Peyser's comparison evoking the controversial Leonard Jeffries is an example of the wrong direction pursued by the press.

Regardless of what one thinks of Leonard Jeffries, he is in fact not part of the same system as Ruth Sherman and her students. While both are tax-levied systems, the City University of New York is not the New York City Board of Education, and Peyser ignores, as have many others, the long and vexing history of Professor Leonard Jeffries and the City College of New York. Peyser's simplistic and deceptive move to conflate the two systems creates the image that there is an institutional mechanism favoring controversial, anti-Semitic blacks over altruistic whites. This manipulative contraction of two different professional and educational domains clouds our view of the institutional mechanisms that were at work to thwart Ruth Sherman's genuine effort to reach out to her students—namely, the curricular, pedagogical, and cultural mechanisms that have historically and institutionally foiled many such efforts.

Contrary to the emotional, fearful, and disoriented-looking woman under attack that the *Post* portrays, *Newsweek* opted for a very different image of Ruth Sherman. The *Newsweek* photograph of Sherman quickly and strikingly erases any trace of a desperate woman in need of help. Instead of the typical black-and-white tabloid shot complete with its traditionally grainy and slightly out-of-focus look, the *Newsweek* photograph has an almost uncanny professional model-shoot look to it. Whereas the *Post* had Sherman on the run, *Newsweek* offers us a very much posed as well as composed, powerful, and sassy-looking woman. Unlike the Sherman looking off into the distance of the *Post*, *Newsweek* has Sherman photographed staring directly into the camera and consequently directly at anyone viewing her. Far from the lost soul adrift in a sea of racial hostility, *Newsweek* has Sherman firmly affixed to the center of her universe. Confident, even defiant, Sherman has the look of a woman in charge, not of someone fleeing for safety.

Oddly enough, however, *Newsweek* chose to present us with this image of Sherman on a bed. Whether it is the bed she normally sleeps in or a bed in a hotel room secured just for the shoot and interview, one can only guess. Regardless of whose bed and bedroom, *Newsweek* gives us then a confident, smartly attired, and supine Sherman with children's books strewn about her. As quickly as *Newsweek* gives us the image of a woman with power, *Newsweek* takes it and sexualizes it by placing this powerful woman on a bed. One has to ask, Why this pose? Why this setting? Of course, one can understand the rationale for transplanting Sherman from the overwrought environs of P.S. 75. But why a bedroom, and why this particular pose? Like a page out of the history of nudes on canvas (and contemporary advertisements), *Newsweek* gives us a representation of Sherman as a woman in control of her position, her place in the world, but strangely enough that place appears to be, according to *Newsweek*, a return to her natural habitat, the bedroom.

Sherman's power then rests in her desirability—that is, as an object of desire. In its attempt to elevate Sherman's status as a star teacher, *Newsweek* reverts to the long-standing cultural norm regarding female desirability—a woman's sex appeal. Apparently, for Sherman to be of any worth, she must have an image consistent with what feminists critically identify as the look of a "real woman." As cultural critic and feminist philosopher Susan Bordo cautions us in "Never Just Pictures," a chapter from her insightful book *Twilight Zones: The Hidden Life of Cultural Images from Plato to O.J.*, we must ever be aware of the lingering sexist notions concerning female power and beauty. This is so, according to Bordo, because, despite the achievements made by women (and men) in the era of what has come to be known as power feminism, "there are old but still operative notions about femininity that subsist alongside the briefcases and Nikes" (Bordo, p. 133). In short, Sherman may have real value as a teacher, but unless she is able to be transposed back into the aesthetics of contemporary normative female beauty, something evidently gets diminished. The story of Ruth Sherman is, based on this logic, of greater importance once we can see that she is the centerfold of this national story and not just its center. Her beauty, her sexiness, her power are all tied to her very white aesthetic, blond hair and all. What gets disguised, denied, and obliterated, then, is the *teacher* Ruth Sherman; what gets promoted is the sexy (idealized) white Ruth Sherman that the parents of color could not tolerate. Thus we are left with the image of a beautiful white woman threatened by the hordes from the mostly black and Hispanic neighborhood. An old story to many, but one the media found worth repeating just the same, and with the repetition of that story, we lose track of the rest of the story.

One important aspect of the story that was ignored was any critical discussion concerning the book *Nappy Hair* itself. Somehow the reporting focused solely on the bald claim that *Nappy Hair* was an unambiguously empowering black pride book. The evidence offered to support this position was presented, in large part, by quoting the book's author, Carolivia Herron. In every case, Herron spoke out in defense of Ruth Sherman and was critical of the dissenting parents. "Children understand that this book is about acceptance and celebration. It pains me that some adults have not gotten there," Herron told *Newsweek*'s Lynette Clemetson. (*Newsweek*, p. 39). In Peyser's article for the *New York Post*, Herron is quoted as saying, "I think it's a marvelous book for giving black children, especially little girls, self-esteem. I'm sorry parents have a problem" (*New York Post*, p. 7). Even the *New York Times* followed a similar strategy. Dinitia Smith of the *Times* quotes Herron sounding equally righteous and complimentary: "Here she [Sherman] was a teacher doing what many don't have the nerve to do, to bring to her students books of their own culture.... I admire what she desired to do" (*New York Times*, p. B10).

This is not to suggest that Carolivia Herron is not an important voice in the debate over the value of her own book. Her words help clarify her intentions and how she believes one might come to embrace the book's message; however, one needs to do more than simply get a green light or an endorsement from the author. In this case, we need to ask why a more critical—not antagonistic—look at the book was left out of the reporting and public debates. We also need to consider how Carolivia Herron, among others, might have been used to diverting discussion away from the difficult issues alluded to above—that is, the difficult cross-cultural and pedogogical issues raised by Sherman's introduction of *Nappy Hair* into her classroom.

In the coverage of the story by Lynette Holloway for the *New York Times*, we get yet another sense of how the debate got pushed in one direction and how Herron became part of the force behind it that pushed. Whereas the *New York Post* and *Newsweek* stories had photographs of Sherman, the *New York Times* opted for a different approach: no photograph of Sherman at all, but rather a photograph of Carolivia Herron set in a separate article inserted into the article about the controversy. The result is a strong, if somewhat distracting, statement of support for Sherman by Herron and other authorities and a less than flattering depiction of the parents.

The title of Holloway's article for the *Times* is straightfoward enough—"School Officials Support Teacher on Book That Parents Call Racially Insensitive" and her reporting is equally to the point:

> New York City school officials yesterday backed a white
> third-grade teacher's use of what black parents asserted
> was a racially insensitive book, but the teacher said she
> feared returning to her classroom because of threats
> from parents. (*New York Times*, November 25, 1998,
> p. B10)

The article goes on to name the various school officials and
representatives who supported Sherman and to criticize the
"parents and community organizers" who challenged the use
of the book. We are told, for example, that

> Mr. Vazquez [the district superintendent] determined
> yesterday that the book, recommended by instructors at
> Teachers College at Columbia University, was not inap-
> propriate.... Ron Davis, a spokesman for the United
> Federation of Teachers, which is assisting Ms. Sherman,
> said the book "was meant to encourage appreciation of
> our cultural diversity and ethnic uniqueness." (Ibid.)

Yet there is no critical evaluation of the book, its merit or
effectiveness for achieving or encouraging "appreciation" of
cultural diversity.

There are, however, assessments of the parents who raised
questions about the book. We are told that

> Isoke T. Nia, the director of research and development at
> the Teachers College Reading and Writing Project at
> Columbia University, who is black, said that she was
> dismayed by the reaction to the book.... "I would like to
> talk to the parents and ask them, 'What is it about your
> hair that you are offended by?' ... There are things that
> blacks say in their homes about their hair and this is
> bringing it to the public," she added. "I'm surprised,
> astonished and appalled...." (Ibid.)

The point is made clearly and strongly in the article that all the experts cited, including the author, are in agreement that the parents "don't get it." We are told by Felix Vazquez, superintendent of District 32, that the book was "recommended for classroom instructors at Teachers College at Columbia University;" that the United Federation of Teachers stood behind Sherman and the book; that Dennis L. Herring, the president of District 32's school board at the time (identified as black in the article), noted that "many people had seen photocopies that gave a false impression of what the illustrations were trying to convey"; and we have Isoke T. Nia, director of Research and Development at the Teachers College Reading and Writing Project (also identified in print as black), expressing her surprise, astonishment, and her being appalled at the parents. We are also offered a biographical article about the book's author, who in addition to being a writer, we are told, has a Ph.D. in comparative literature from an Ivy League school, is former director of the Epicenter for the Study of Oral Poetry at Harvard, and is currently a professor of English in California. All of these people are knowledgeable and credible. There is, therefore, no problem with *Nappy Hair*; it is the ignorant parents and overactive community organizers who have the problem. The experts have spoken: They are black and Hispanic, so there's no need to go farther. What's left undiscussed, of course, is the book itself and the pedagogical implications of cross-cultural interactions, especially concerning a sensitive issue such as "nappy hair."

Sadly, when the issue of the cultural significance of nappy hair finally does make its way into the debate it surfaces as yet further proof that the entire controversy is a "black problem," not an education issue per se, and certainly not Ruth Sherman's problem. Writing for the *New York Times*'s op-ed page a few days after the story broke, Jill Nelson, author of *Straight No Chaser: How I Became a Grown-up Black Woman*, noted that

[w]hile Ms. Sherman understood her students' need for positive self-images, it's clear she had no inkling that sometimes barriers to that self-esteem *are perpetuated not by the white community but by the black one.* (*New York Times*, November 28, 1998, p. A15; emphasis added)

Nelson's point is that Sherman (and subsequently the rest of the white community) "stumbled onto a volatile race secret and uncovered a strain of self-hatred in African-American culture that in this instance made education an explosive issue." (Ibid.) She concludes by exclaiming,

[t]hat some read the writer's words as an insult is neither the writer's problem nor the teacher's. It is an issue that must be dealt with by *those* who use "nappy" not as a description but as an epithet and then attack the messengers who dare challenge their destructive attitudes. (Ibid. emphasis added.)

Of course, the point is that "those" in question are African Americans themselves, so we come full circle: An African-American scholar writes a book that is troubling to African Americans who use "nappy" as an epithet and then get outraged when a white school teacher uses the book to promote self-esteem.

The problem with this analysis, though it is more probing than that of other articles, is that it, too, seeks to exonerate Sherman's naïvité and her lack of education in cross-cultural dynamics and refuses to address the possibility that the book *Nappy Hair* is not necessarily the best vehicle to use for building self-esteem. Those wanting to write off the entire controversy as little more than ungrateful, ignorant, and now self-hating parents of color venting their rage at an innocent white do-gooder have the complete story they need to justify their position. That the author and other qualified African Americans essentially blame the parents makes it all the easier to simplify everything as a "black problem" and not a pedagogical one, which would make it Ruth Sherman's problem, along with every other teacher working in similar circumstances.

The claim here is not that Ruth Sherman ought to be blamed or that *Nappy Hair* is an example of self-hatred, but rather that Ruth Sherman was most likely not offered the important concepts and tools in her teacher preparation program to deal with such issues and that *Nappy Hair* may not be the straightforward narrative of self-esteem that everyone defending it assumes or claims. It is important, therefore, to look at the book in some detail and consider the importance of a genuinely multicultural approach to teaching, an approach not necessarily or automatically employed by merely reading from a so-called culturally relevant book.

Nappy Hair was published by Dragonfly Books, an imprint of Alfred A. Knopf, in 1997. As is true for many children's books, the story is accompanied by illustrations. In this instance, Carolivia Herron collaborated with illustrator Joe Cepeda to produce *Nappy Hair*. It is a playfully written and colorfully illustrated book; *Nappy Hair* is also a book with a message. This is clear even before we read the story. On the inside cover, the publisher emphasizes the potential of the story by offering "A Note to Parents and Teachers," suggesting fun activities "inspired by the story." We are also informed that all of this special attention is part of what the publisher calls the "Dragonfly Difference," the claim that Dragonfly Books go the extra step or two to provide more for their readers (and in this case their readers' parents and teachers).

We are presented with the "Dragonfly Sing Along," which explains the "call and response" style of Herron's narrative and encourages readers to participate in the fun of this style of writing by taking turns reading out loud the various "calls" and "responses." There is also the "Dragonfly Write Idea," an activity involving the participants in completing "the sentences below with the right words." We are given a few incomplete sentences, such as "Sarah's hair is as soft as . . . ," "John's nose is as small as . . . ," along with choices to complete the sentences—for example, silk, a button, and so on. After successfully finishing the activity, readers are further encouraged to write their own sentences about the way they look.

On the back inside cover we have "Dragonfly Family Fun," asking readers to remember family gatherings (such as the picnic that takes place in *Nappy Hair*), and to "draw pictures of a past family gathering or celebration that would be fun to have in the future." Finally there are "Dragonfly Descriptions," instructing readers to "look at yourself in a mirror," then "write a short paragraph describing your special qualities." It is obvious from even just a cursory look at the book and its "suggested activities" that it is intended to be a fun book for learning. So what went wrong?

Upon a closer look, *Nappy Hair* is no simple story. We are told that "at a backyard picnic" Uncle Mordecai told a story, that all "the folks joined in between the lines, little Jimmy taped it, and here it is" (p. 1). Without going into a full-scale literary analysis based on contemporary theories of narrative construction, it is, nevertheless, worth mentioning that the reader is immediately presented with an interesting, if not confusing, narrative and setting. The story was told by Uncle Mordecai, the story was taped by little Jimmy, and "here it is."

We are confronted by a rather complex and vague timeline. That is, the temporality, if you will, of the narrative is rendered somewhat unstable by virtue of the fact that the story was told, the story was taped, and yet "here it is." Where is it? Is it when it was told? Is it a replaying of the tape made by little Jimmy? And if so, how long ago was it taped, and does that matter? Are we listening to the tape now or are we now in the very moment (in the past) when the story was told and being taped?

The questions continue. Where are we? Are we at the picnic, or somewhere and at some time far removed from Uncle Mordecai and "the folks [who] joined in between the lines?" What do we make of this setting and details? Is the taping a metaphor of the need to document what families, what black families, say and think? Is the book *Nappy Hair* itself such a taping, an archival document intended to preserve and testify to such speech and family conversations? Is this what Isoke T. Nia was alluding to when she rebuked the parents from P.S. 75 in the *New York Times* with her challenge "'What is it about your hair that you are offended by? There are things that blacks say in their homes about their hair and [*Nappy Hair*] is bringing it to the public." Is there some imperative to record and repeat the things that are said? Should the private interactions taking place at family gatherings and celebrations become part of a larger and more public (political) discourse? All these many questions are provoked from just the six lines on the first page of *Nappy Hair*.

Of course, one could argue that such a perspective is overly complicated and academic, in the pejorative sense. It is, after all, just a children's story, so why overanalyze these relatively simple lines. Certainly we should not ask the children reading this book, or even the parents reading it to them, to consider such questions. But is it really unfair to ask those teachers and scholars who use and recommend this kind of book to look this carefully at something to be introduced into the curriculum and lives of students? That *Nappy Hair* is simply a story told by Uncle Mordecai is clear enough; however, how the story is being told and/or retold cannot be unimportant. If it were unimportant, why did the author go to such effort to put things together the way she did? Why bother with the details of who told the story and how it was recorded? One can only assume that Carolivia Herron thought things through and decided that the timeline and style she chose were in fact important. So why would one shy away from discussing the style or narrative structure of the story, especially if they help or hinder the ostensible goal of promoting self-esteem?

But if forced to, we could forgo such a discussion and still question the claim that *Nappy Hair* is an unambiguously straightforward story promoting self-esteem, a story that everyone "gets," save the oversensitive, ignorant, and self-hating parents of P.S. 75. We could, for example, do one of the recommended activities suggested by the publisher, let's say a "Dragonfly Description."

This activity is broken up into two distinct parts. First we are told that

> Uncle Mordecai's descriptions turn Brenda's willful hair into a symbol of her history, her heritage and her own strength. What words does Uncle Mordecai use to describe Brenda's hair? What wonderful things does he say about Brenda? (*Nappy Hair*, inside back cover)

Then, secondly, we are told to

> [l]ook at yourself in the mirror. Do you have hair like Brenda's—or is it completely different? What is your favorite part about looking the way you do? Write a short paragraph describing your special qualities. Attach a photograph of yourself to the paragraph. Keep it for yourself—or send it to a friend or relative who lives far away. (Ibid.)

The directions are easy to understand and sound like fun. The first part is an excellent activity for reinforcing reading comprehension and appreciation of the details of the story. The second part is equally positive-sounding and, on the surface, is an activity promoting self-awareness and self-esteem.

For obvious reasons we will not pursue the second part of the activity but will consider the first. "What words does Uncle Mordecai use to describe Brenda's hair? What wonderful things does he say about Brenda?" What things, indeed?

Immediately following the introduction to the story are Uncle Mordecai's words (p. 3). Page two has a pleasant depiction of a smiling, gray-haired Uncle Mordecai sitting in a rocking chair on a back porch. He is speaking, "calling out" to Brenda and a woman (Brenda's mother, aunt, neighbor?) holding a casserole dish of some type. Uncle Mordecai calls out: "Brenda, you sure do got some nappy hair on your head, don't you?" (*Nappy Hair*, p. 3). The response is a not so simple "Well," written in big letters, for emphasis. But the reply clearly indicates that Uncle Mordecai has gotten everyone's attention, and there is an air of guarded anticipation about where all this is going. Given that we are attempting to catalog "what wonderful things" Uncle Mordecai says about Brenda, I will not include the responses each time but will from time to time to further elaborate on a particular point.

Uncle Mordecai continues: "It's your hair, Brenda, take the cake.... And come back and get the plate." On the next pages (4 and 5), Uncle Mordecai is shown standing, holding Brenda in one hand and holding his walking cane high above his head, addressing the family members gathered at the picnic table in the backyard. We can see a smiling Brenda petting a dog, seemingly unaware of or not concerned with Uncle Mordecai's words. The rest of the group, including little Jimmy with his tape recorder, however, appear to be very attentive to what Uncle Mordecai is saying, even apprehensive. Everyone seems frozen still. The woman holding the casserole dish from the previous page is still holding the dish and looking intently toward Uncle Mordecai; others have interrupted a card game to turn and give Uncle Mordecai their full attention; there is even a little girl under the table looking up and out toward Uncle Mordecai. Everyone, save Brenda, is anxiously waiting for what words will follow.

"It ain't easy to come by that kind of hair" (p. 4), he says. "You just can't blame Africa. It's willful" (p. 5), he exclaims. And with this Carolivia Herron sets the stage for presenting us with the message that Brenda's hair was intended to be that way. Later in the narrative, we find out that God has willed Brenda's hair to be so nappy. In the end, we are given a wonderful message, that an all-powerful and all-loving God created Brenda and her nappy hair. What more proof do we need that Brenda and her hair are things of beauty?

I believe that this is the message Carolivia Herron set out to bring to all who read her book, but let's continue to examine what Uncle Mordecai says about Brenda. On page 6 we are told that combing Brenda's hair is "like scrunching through the New Mexico desert in brogans in the heat of summer." Uncle Mordecai's descriptions continue on page 8, where he tells us that "It's like crunching through snow." "Y'all know how it sounds when you scrunching through snow like that? That's what her hair sounds like when she comb it out in the morning." The illustration accompanying this portion of the narrative is of Brenda and Uncle Mordecai working their way through some deep, crunchy snow. Again it is clear that the image is meant to be playful and lighthearted. Yet the response to all of this by those listening is, "Brother, you ought to be ashamed," meaning ashamed of so graphically (and unmercifully?) describing Brenda's nappy hair.

This is where some of the confusion concerning the intent of the book may lie. You have, on the one hand, an important but subtle message being expressed: Since Brenda's hair is so willfully nappy and, as we later find out, that it is God's will itself that is the cause of this hair, Brenda and her hair are facto things of beauty. On the other hand, we have the harsh words and descriptions coming from Uncle Mordecai that even his own family members believe to be shameful; as they put it, "Brother, you ought to be ashamed." This split, this tension is the heart and soul of *Nappy Hair*, and I believe with the appropriate work and commentary, the message of pride and beauty can shine through; however, this is not automatic.

The next lines following the family's response—that he ought to be ashamed—express Uncle Mordecai's love for and pride in Brenda. Uncle Mordecai counters the response exhorting shame with a passionate and bold reply: "Ashamed? I'm not ashamed. I'm proud. She's the only one in her school knows how to talk right." He goes on to tell us that she is "A rose among a thousand thorns" and that "Them old hardheads think they can talk English. But this chile talks the king's English. Talk the queen's English too" (Herron, p. 10). Across the page and these powerful lines of praise and acknowledgment is an illustration of an animated and joyous Brenda reciting something to her class. Brenda is clearly on top of the world, enjoying her moment in front of the class.

The problem with this is precisely the shift from the harsh words concerning her hair and therefore her looks, to the effusive expression of pride in her ability to speak both the king's and the queen's English. This is confusing, in part because of the move from looks to intellect and ability, an ability "to talk right" at that. If the pride Uncle Mordecai has for Brenda is, at least so far, based on her skill to speak properly, does this mean that Brenda is okay as long as she demonstrates her ability (her willingness) to conform, in this case to speak the king's and the queen's English (standard English)? What message has the book clearly established so far? We are eleven pages into a thirty-one-page story, a third of the way through the narrative, and at this point the message is complex and perhaps even ambivalent: Uncle Mordecai clearly expresses his pride in Brenda, a pride thus far based on her ability to "talk right"; but he has also stated some strong words concerning her hair that cause family members listening to him to exclaim their discomfort with all this talk about Brenda's hair.

Is *Nappy Hair*, then, not a book encouraging self-esteem and pride? This is not the point. As already noted, with the appropriate setting up and commentary, *Nappy Hair* can prove to be a powerful narrative about Brenda, Uncle Mordecai, history, family togetherness, love, and beauty; the point, however, is that all this may be the case, but it is hardly unambiguously or unproblematically so. Given the racism that exists, the issues surrounding Black English, and the history of undermining the self-esteem of people of color in the classroom, is it unfair to demand a critical discussion about the appropriateness of using *Nappy Hair* in any class-room setting without attention to the issues raised here? There are tensions, legitimate ones, that Herron forces her readers to address; the question is, are these complicated and emotionally charged themes presented so flawlessly and straightforwardly that all who read this book must get its positive message unless they are overreactive, self-hating individuals? I think not.

If we resume following Uncle Mordecai's narrative, he returns, after his brief moment of praise, with comments about Brenda's hair, much to the consternation of those listening. Uncle Mordecai continues: "But she sure, Lord, got some nappy hair on her head." The family replies, "Now, why's he got to come back to that?" If one stopped reading at this point, even with the intention of continuing later, perhaps another day, the wonderful things Uncle Mordecai has thus far said do not add up to very much. If you also consider the give-and-take of the narrative, calls and responses, it is not an exaggeration to say that the book is struggling within itself. The fact that Herron continues the narrative in a direction that, I would agree, is positive and promotes pride, doesn't mean that she does so in the manner that the media suggested in the coverage of the Ruth Sherman incident, namely that *Nappy Hair* is, beyond any question, a black pride book.

All sorts of questions need to be asked. For example, when reading this book out loud, should white teachers speak the Black English it is written in, without hesitation, without any explanation? Should teachers of color read it this way? What does it mean for a teacher to read in such a manner to any group of students but especially students of color and students who speak English as a second language? Did Ruth Sherman do any preparatory work of this sort? Did she consult with any teachers of color about her lesson? These were the questions never asked by the media, and one suspects they weren't asked by Sherman either. From all that she stated to the media, she was simply reading a story, one that she believed her students could relate to. But in a cultural, political, and historical context that is so charged with tensions and sensitivities about race and status, aren't such questions mandatory for anyone teaching today? However well intended, the inclusion of a "culturally relevant" book does not free us from the important work needed when using such a book. Such discussions, such work, make all the difference and should be rigorously explored at every stage of a teacher's career.

Nappy Hair is an important book because of the serious message Carolivia Herron presents, that Brenda's nappy hair is an act of God's will and love. Brenda and all like her are therefore symbols of God's infinite creation and love and must be treated with the respect that all such beings deserve. But *Nappy Hair* is not necessarily an easy book to read (emotionally or intellectually) for the reasons we have been discussing.

None of this is to say that the parents of P.S. 75 were right about Ruth Sherman's values and her desire to teach, only that there was and remains much more to the story than the media chose to explore at the time, including the issue of introducing God into a class lesson in a public school.

In 1999, writer and critic bell hooks (also an African American) published her first children's book, *Happy to Be Nappy*, with Jump at the Sun, an imprint of Hyperion Books for Children. This poem-story stands in stark contrast to *Nappy Hair*. Rather than adopt the complex narrative style and content of Carolivia Herron's book, bell hooks chose to present an unproblematic and straightforward celebration of a little girl and her hair. The poem begins: "Girlpie hair smells clean . . . and sweet" (hooks, pp. 2, 3). Though bell hooks also chose to use Black English, we immediately notice the difference between the overall tone and mood of *Nappy Hair* and *Happy to Be Nappy*. First, there is no complex narrative or timeline; instead we are greeted by the simple, soft, and pleasant words that "Girlpie hair smells clean . . . and sweet." Second, and perhaps most important, there is no Uncle Mordecai and his important but, by comparison, far more complicated (sometimes troubling) words of love and pride.

Happy to Be Nappy is about "girlpie" first and foremost. True, as is the case with *Nappy Hair*, there are the grand concepts of black pride, love, and beauty. But bell hooks, often identified with her sharp-tongued criticism of what she calls "white-supremist, capitalist, patriarchy," here offers us gentle, comforting, and welcoming words about girlpie and her hair. Girlpie's hair "is soft like cotton, flower petal billowy soft, full of frizz and fuzz" (Ibid., pp. 3, 4). These evocative, poetic words are a far cry from the inflammatory inaugural comments made by Uncle Mordecai. The narrator of *Happy to Be Nappy*, whoever she might be, speaks directly to the reader and makes sure that her message of love and praise sings out from every page, every line, and every word. Girlpie's hair is "A halo—a crown—a covering for heads that are round" (Ibid., pp. 5, 6).

It may be that *Happy to Be Nappy* lacks the cosmological implications of *Nappy Hair*, but the point is simply that if one is going to read a book to kids and use it to promote self-esteem and disrupt traditional racist notions about beauty and aesthetic values in general, then might not we do better to use a text that *clearly* embraces the character and themes being presented? *Nappy Hair* will no doubt continue be part of the curriculum, so we must remain responsible and diligent regarding how and when such a book is to be used. It is, after all, one thing to try to explain the profound metaphysical connections to be made among Brenda's hair, God, and all things good and beautiful; it is still another to just sing out loudly and clearly that one is happy to be nappy.

3.

From Substandard to Nonstandard English

Getting beyond the Morality of Speaking Right

In 1999 I was invited to give a talk to participants in a special program designed for Ivy League students interested in urban education and considering careers as teachers. The group, I was told, was particularly intelligent and sophisticated, so I should be prepared to speak about something challenging, stimulating, and related to their student teaching.

I began my talk by suggesting that there were many issues that could be the focus of a presentation concerning urban education: overcrowded classrooms, disruptive students, bilingual education, truancy, and remediation, to name just a few of the frequently discussed topics. But I wanted, I told them, to address a somewhat less familiar issue for this occasion, one that focused on the attitude of teachers toward the "standard English" debate. Specifically, I wanted to explore with this group of bright and dedicated student teachers their attitudes and feelings concerning their students (and people generally) who speak or write nonstandard English.

The group immediately and enthusiastically responded to my inquiry. They emphasized the importance of speaking properly to get ahead in our society. "One needs to be able to communicate in the business world by speaking properly," one participant said. Another seconded this opinion by adding, "Our students will never get a good job if they speak Black

English or demonstrate an inferior understanding or command of the English language." I expressed my agreement with their overall assessment of the realities of communicating in the business world, and other domains where standard English is in fact "the standard." But I reminded them that I was interested in what *they* felt about nonstandard usage, not what the callous world of commerce might demand. For a moment or two there was a slightly awkward silence before someone said, "I hadn't really thought about it, I mean what I actually feel about it, but I guess I kind of think that substandard English is a problem for everyone, educationally and culturally." Others quickly joined in. "I agree," said another participant. "I am always spending time correcting my students' speech, telling them that the classroom requires standard English and they will suffer academically and socially if they don't start using it."

The faculty member who coordinated the program rightly looked on with a sense of pride: her students were not going to back away from the challenge of offering all children the opportunity to succeed. It was imperative that students, especially urban students of color, learn to use standard English. "It is, after all," she asserted, "the most agreed upon-view of what is the appropriate way to speak; that's why we call it standard and other ways of speaking substandard." What followed was a lengthy, challenging, and judging by the dynamics of the conversation, a stimulating interaction. Although I acknowledged the obvious commitment of the student teachers to helping urban students get ahead and the importance of standard English, I argued for the need to abandon the use of the traditional opposition of "standard versus substandard" when describing the different forms of spoken English in the United States. I claimed that such a perspective was ultimately pedagogically suspect and linguistically unjustified, at best somewhat patronizing and misleading and at worst alienating and false. I suggested that there should be a greater recognition of the significance of switching to a view that emphasized a distinction between standard and nonstandard forms of our language, as an alternative to the traditional (political) opposition. The coordinator of the program protested this kind of move. She argued that such a switch was not particularly helpful because it implied that the old "opposition" was merely political and that to make such a claim would undermine the importance of standard English and speaking right, something teachers cannot risk or afford in their fight to educate students, especially urban students of color. I expressed my hope that more teachers would someday take such risks because their students cannot afford for them not to do so.

The stance of arguing for and protecting the value and appropriateness of standard English, though often predicated on the admirable goal of better serving children, especially children of color, is, in large part, the reason why there are so many harsh and volatile debates over the use of nonstandard English (as well as that of bilingualism) in and out of the classroom. It is neither my goal to debunk the significance of standard English in any way, nor to suggest that students need not achieve a certain level of competency, if not mastery of it. On the contrary, I am an advocate of teaching standard English and assisting all citizens, not just young ones, in gaining fluency in this globally important language. But my concerns now, as was true when I addressed that group of promising student teachers participating in the special program, are: What are the reasons, justifications, and attitudes at play in promoting standard English? What are the values underlying the teaching of standard English in the first place? Might we move more successfully toward the goal of teaching students this form of English if we first look at our attitudes, then make the appropriate strategic shifts to better serve this goal?

The responses from both the student teachers and the coordinator of their program that day suggest, when all is said and done, that the motivation propelling the teaching of standard English, for many people, is more a moral imperative than an educational one per se. In short, the reason why many believe that standard English must be taught is due to its inherent superiority and value over other, "substandard" forms of the language. The students and their coordinator voiced their acceptance of this position when they made the justifiable connections linking success, business, and standard English. They took it as a given that other, "substandard" forms of English would hurt one's chances to succeed in our culture. They did not, however, consider challenging the politics or ethics of this condition, but rather accepted the alleged superiority of standard English, and therefore its greater usefulness and appropriateness, over all other forms of the language. I want to abandon the "standard versus substandard" opposition, which assumes and advocates the superiority of the standard form over the "substandard," and embrace the "standard and nonstandard" distinction as a more accurate description of the difference at play here. By doing so, we can move away from the morality of speaking right, and move toward a pragmatics of speaking standard English. I want to argue that this distinction is actually more supportive of the ethical and political reasons why anyone living in the United States today ought to engage in learning and speaking standard English, if not exclusively, then certainly in addition to any other language or nonstandard form of English. It is my claim that switching to such a distinction to describe the English spoken in the United States will promote a more positive and effective pedagogy.

As I will discuss later in this chapter, the primary ethical reason for using the standard/nonstandard distinction and for teaching standard English is to promote and enhance democracy in our country. *This* ethical imperative must be the force behind the teaching and learning of standard English. The self-righteous indignation and demeaning condescension toward those who speak a nonstandard form of English, or another language altogether, have led to bad pedagogy in an antidemocratic spirit. This undermines the very strengthening of our nation that so many adherents of the morality of speaking right long for at this historical moment. This is why the debate, as it is currently framed, is about politics and power in the narrow sense, and not meaningful educative strategies. It is also why there is a genuine political need to shift the debate toward gaining an understanding of the full cultural, and ultimately ethical, reasons for accepting the standard-nonstandard distinction and lay to rest, once and for all, the presumed moral superiority of standard English over something called substandard English. My position throughout this book is that acting on ethical principles is fundamentally different from the mere imposition of dominant (that is to say, mainstream but subject to political, even contradictory, manipulation) moral values of a given cultural moment. I believe that pursuing an ethical rather than merely moral position concerning the dynamics of language will lead to better teaching and greater success for students.

In the introduction to her provocative book *Talking Power: The Politics of Language*, linguist Robin Tolmach Lakoff boldly states that

> [l]anguage is politics, politics assigns power, power governs how people talk and how they are understood. The analysis of language from this point of view is more than an academic exercise: today, more than ever, it is a survival skill. (p. 7)

That language is understood in the context of political power and survival is not a contemporary notion. One could trace this connection back to numerous traditions quite easily. In the Western tradition, for example, even a quick look at any number of the philosopher Plato's "dialogues" can offer us proof of the significance, for him, between language and political power.

Plato's *Apology* is perhaps one of the most moving and graphic examples of this relationship. Socrates addresses the Athenian court in his own defense and reminds his judges, made up of fellow Athenian citizens, that

> [t]his is my first appearance in a court of law, at the age of seventy, and so I am a complete stranger to the language of this place. Now if I were really from another country, you would naturally excuse me if I spoke in the manner and dialect in which I had been brought up, and so in the present case I make this request of you, which I think is only reasonable, to disregard the manner of my speech— it may be better or worse—and to consider and concentrate your attention upon this one question, whether my claims are fair or not. (p. 4)

For the historical Socrates this certainly was no mere academic exercise; he was defending himself against a charge that would eventually demand his life for the penalty.

Other examples of the claim that there exists an inextricable relationship among language, power, politics, and survival can be readily found in numerous stories in the Bible. The Tower of Babel in the Book of Genesis makes this connection particularly clear.

> And they said one to another, Go to, let us build us a city and a tower, whose top may reach unto heaven; and let us make us a name, lest we be scattered abroad upon the face of the whole earth.
>
> And the Lord, came down to see the city and the tower, which the children of men builded.

And the Lord said, Behold, the people is one, and they have all one language; and this they begin to do: and now nothing will be restrained from them, which they have imagined to do.

Go to, let us go down, and there confound their language, that they may not understand one another's speech.

So the Lord scattered them abroad from thence upon the face of all the earth; and they left off to build the city.

Therefore is the name of it called Babel; because the Lord did there confound the language of the earth. (Genesis 11:4–9)

So language, one might argue, has long been, if not always been, connected to power, politics, and survival. This connection, if not universal, is made by many cultures throughout history.

In pre-Columbian America we are finding out that the kings and ruling class of the Mayan civilization were well aware of the relationship between language and power. In a *New York Times* "Science Times" article of July, 17, 2001, John Noble Wilford reports that

> kings fervently, perhaps desperately, believed in the power of the pen. . . . [A] growing body of evidence from Maya writing and art shows that scribes played a central role in magnifying their king's reputation and solidifying his political hold on the realm. (p. F1)

Quoting Dr. Kevin J. Johnson, an archaeologist at Ohio State University specializing in Mayan culture, Wilford further notes that the texts generated by scribes "were a medium through which kings asserted and displayed power" (Ibid., p. F2).

That contemporary Americans witness this connection among language, power, politics, and survival almost every day in dramatic and less dramatic fashion does not always lead, it appears, to a critical stance toward language, power, and politics. (One wonders how long former president Clinton's infamous utterance concerning the verb "is" in responding to allegations of a sexual relationship will continue to be the exemplar of political power and manipulation, or how long before the Republican Party rhetoric controlling the Florida voting debacle during the presidential election of 2000 completely fades from the national memory.) Thus it is not so surprising that many different sectors of American culture have naively joined forces to protect the status of standard English in the United States.

For many teachers, cultural commentators, and conservative politicians, there is a presumption about the very nature of standard English, that it is worth protecting because of its inherent linguistic value and not because of power and politics. This is where we must begin to argue for the adoption of the standard/nonstandard distinction. We must do this on two fronts: First, it must be reiterated that standard English *is* a political as well as a linguistic institution, and a political institution "imposed" by a political "victor" on the diverse peoples who did, do, and will inhabit the United States; and second, that the nature of language is not what many of the advocates of standard English believe, namely that the grammatical rules, pronunciations, and vocabulary got somehow magically created and now are eternally fixed and free from change from the dynamics of power and politics. These two dimensions of the argument need to be understood if real progress is going to be made in the teaching and learning of standard English, something, I repeat, I am in favor of because of its significance for democracy to work well in the United States.

It is certainly harsh words to the ears of many patriotic citizens to hear that standard English is the language of an oppressor—the native tongue, if you will, of the increasingly vilified white Anglo-Saxon Protestant male. Yet even a superficial consideration of the history of the United States—and the rest of the world, for that matter (New, Old, or Third)—makes it abundantly clear that languages do not simply get adopted in a vacuum, but emerge from the violent realities of political and cultural conquests. Bluntly put, this is why Portuguese is spoken in Brazil and not Spanish, why Spanish is spoken in Mexico and not Dutch, why French is still spoken in Morocco, Algeria, and other countries in Africa in addition to Arabic and numerous other African languages, and why English is spoken in India, the United States, and Canada, and also is the reason why the Québec Province in Canada is waging a cultural and political struggle for French. It is about power—who has it and who does not. This is the political and historical context in which teaching and learning standard English take place. This is why we must reevaluate the pedagogy of speaking right, a pedagogy for many understood as speaking *white*.

Given this history and these circumstances, characterizing standard English as a political institution as well as a linguistic one could be considered redundant, as could be the case for so many other languages, if not all of them. But such a characterization ought not distract us, as it has many others, with attempts to justify or belittle the significance of this cultural fact. Instead, we ought to understand this cultural/political/linguistic history more fully to be better prepared for teaching standard English to many who experience this history, in many different ways, every time they talk and identify themselves as nonstandard speakers. For some, continuing to speak nonstandard English is a conscious decision to resist being "converted" or overpowered by the dominant white culture, while for others their continued use is based on habit, familiarity, and successful communicative acts within their communities. In either case an appeal (often a demand) to switch to standard English cannot be made based on its superiority or use value alone. Such a strategy ignores political reality and denies the actual benefits of speaking nonstandard English. In the former case it only serves to further alienate and antagonize the speakers of nonstandard English, and in the latter case it flies in the face of lived experience, which testifies to the value of nonstandard English. The results are greater hostility and confusion, not greater acceptance of standard English.

In his classic analysis titled *Blues People: The Negro Experience in White America and the Music That Developed from It*, Amiri Baraka (formerly LeRoi Jones) offers us this analogy and assessment:

> If you are taken to Mongolia as a slave and work there seventy-five years and learn twenty words of Mongolian and live in a small house from which you leave only to work, I don't think we can call you a Mongolian. It is only when you begin to accept the idea that you are part of that country that you can be said to be a permanent resident. I mean, that until the time when you have sufficient ideas about this new country to begin making some lasting moral generalizations about it—relating your experience, in some lasting form in the language of that country, with whatever subtleties and obliqueness you bring to it—you are merely a transient. There were no formal stories about the Negro's existence in America passed down in any pure African tongue. The stories, myths, moral examples, etc., given in African were about Africa. When America became important to the African to be passed on, in those formal renditions, to the young, those renditions were in some kind of Afro-American language. And finally, when a man looked up in some anonymous field and shouted, "Oh, Ahm tired a dis mess, / Oh, yes Ahm so tired a dis mess," you can be sure he was an American. (p. xiii)

The birth of the Afro-American language referred to here punctuates a new identity and subjectivity, a consciousness that resides as a "permanent resident." Such a language, such a bond of humanity at such a moment of inhumanity is why standard English cannot be offered (and certainly not demanded) to be accepted as a simple nonpolitical superior substitute for Black English. The history of this form of nonstandard English is too significant for its speakers, too profoundly bound to their identity *as* Americans, to be simply abandoned or designated "substandard" by a cultural elite claiming the superiority of their language.

Those involved in teaching, but especially in the teaching of standard English, must begin to fully recognize the significance of the cultural, historical, and political reality of Black English and its speakers. To ignore these realities is to refuse to accept American history and the consquences of the black diaspora. As James Baldwin pointedly wrote in a 1979 letter to the editor of the *New York Times* ("If Black Isn't a Language, Then Tell Me, What Is It?"):

Black English is the creation of the Black Diaspora. Blacks came to the United States chained to each other, but from different tribes: Neither could speak the other's language. If two Black people at that bitter hour of the world's history, had been able to speak to each other, the institution of chattel slavery could never have lasted as long as it did. Subsequently, the slave was given, under the eye, and the gun, of his master, Congo Square, and the Bible—or, in other words, and under these conditions, the slave began the formation of the Black church, and it is within this unprecedented tabernacle that Black English began to be formed. This was not merely, as in the European example, the adoption of a foreign tongue, but an alchemy that transformed ancient elements into new language: *A language comes into existence by means of brutal necessity, and the rules of the language are dictated by what the language must convey.* (p. 69)

Whatever pedagogical approach is to be employed in teaching standard English, it is necessary, if not obvious, to incorporate and acknowledge the history and cultural significance of Black English as a nonstandard form of particular merit, linguistically and politically. All teachers ought to be required to know this history and to be educated about the linguistic and cultural importance of this major nonstandard form of English. This should be so, not to artificially inflate the value of Black English, but rather to formally and appropriately acknowledge, to answer Baldwin, what it is.

Given their assessments of the status of Black English—its cultural, historical, *and* linguistic significance—Amiri Baraka and James Baldwin make the case for the need to reevaluate the attitudes and values of those arguing for the superiority of standard English. The need becomes even more salient for educators who must challenge the demonization and delegitimization of Black English. This challenge becomes a fundamental step toward understanding the validity of this nonstandard form of English and a necessary step toward good pedagogy. To do otherwise is bad history, bad linguistics, bad teaching, and, in light of the analysis offered here, is also unethical. I say unethical because to do otherwise harms many students and harms our democracy in the process. By continuing to maintain that Black English is linguistically and morally inferior, advocates of standard English do harm to the well-being of our nation. For those who would claim that such an assertion is more histrionic than valid history, I counter with this simple yet bold question: On what linguistic principles and cultural history does standard English enjoy its status over Black English?

Theresa Perry and Lisa Delpit, coeditors of *The Real*

Ebonics Debate: Power, Language, and the Education of African-American Children, lay out the entire debate in their powerful and pursuasive collection of essays on the subject. These two scholars map out the terrain of the Black English debate by focusing on the controversy that erupted over the Oakland School Board's resolution, passed in December 1996 during Kwanza, to have teachers become more knowledgable about Black English and more fully aware of the historical/political/cultural context in which it is spoken. Their anthology should be required reading for all teachers, but especially those working with African-American students.

What Perry and Delpit offer is, in essence, a case study of the historical, political, cultural, and linguistic context of Black English. Their book successfully answers the questions of what teachers need to know and what they can do to help their students. They and their contributors argue for the value of standard English, yet insist on the need to give speakers of Black English the opportunity, the freedom to express themselves in the language that is so important to African-American culture.

But I want to go still further with this issue. I want to be clear that it is not simply a matter of "allowing" nonstandard speakers of English, especially of Black English, the chance to gain a little political ground, important as this may be. I want to insist that teachers must have a more comprehensive knowledge of the dynamics of language and the role that standard English plays in our democracy. This is to ensure a greater possibility of academic success along with genuine recognition of the value of nonstandard forms of English and their users, our fellow citizens and neighbors.

As noted earlier, many have written on the relationship of power and language. What makes the issue of Black English of particular concern is the attempt to subordinate it (and its speakers) in our schools and our democracy. This, to repeat myself, is not to suggest that standard English be relegated to some less significant role but rather that all involved in education should have a more sophisticated understanding and a less moralistic attitude toward it and nonstandard forms. To be sure, my own attitudes and values could (and should) be questioned, but it strikes me that the inherent antidemocratic nature of the standard English debate demands the sort of discussion I am offering here.

Although my own attitudes toward language, power, and politics are informed by a tradition that stretches from philosophers such as Plato, Hegel, Heidegger, and Derrida, and literary critics such as M. M. Baktin, Harold Bloom, and Terry Eagleton, and cultural critics including bell hooks, one does not need this list of theorists to come to some simple but essential positions concerning language in general and standard English in particular. For example, in his best-selling book *The Mother Tongue: English and How It Got That Way*, Bill Bryson notes

> English grammar is so complex and confusing for the one very simple reason that its rules and terminology are based on Latin—a language with which it has precious little in common. In Latin, to take one example, it is not possible to split an infinitive. So in English, the early authorities decided, it should not be possible to split an infinitive either. But there is no reason why we shouldn't, any more than we should forsake instant coffee and air travel because they weren't available to the Romans. Making English grammar conform to Latin rules is like asking people to play baseball using the rules of football. It is patent absurdity. But once this insane notion became established grammarians found themselves having to draw up ever more complicated and circular arguments to accommodate the inconsistencies. As Burchfield notes

in *The English Language*, one authority, F. Th. Visser, found it necessary to devote 200 pages to discussing just one aspect of the present participle. That is as crazy as it is amazing. (p. 137)

Crazy and amazing indeed, yet for many earnest speakers of English, this maze of rules and regulations stands as a foundational pillar of our civilization itself. As such, people just assume the linguistic and moral authority of these rules and regulations, frowning on those who neither understand nor properly employ them.

In just the one section quoted above from Bill Bryson's book there is a wealth of material to begin challenging many of the long-standing attitudes surrounding standard English, the first being that all the rules of standard English make linguistic sense, as opposed to reflecting the cultural and political attitudes of those involved in formulating and enforcing these grammatical positions. If more teachers, and all those for whom standard English represents an educational high-water mark that must be reached by all students, could begin to see this one issue clearly, free from the haze that clouds their vision, then we could truly begin talking about the pragmatics of standard English and finally get beyond the morality of speaking right.

What most teachers, along with the average speaker of standard English, rightly assume is that the English spoken today is the result of years of development and codification. What most are unaware of, or choose to ignore, is the actual history of that development and codification. By studying the history of standard English, teachers would learn useful information and concepts that would help in the teaching of the language. But this history also would reveal what has already been noted above, namely, that the presumption of the intrinsic linguistic and moral superiority needs to be abandoned.

The challenge is to give up a rigid (and often antagonistic) adherence to "prescriptivism," a view of language that has been around for a long time.

The British linguist David Crystal succinctly describes prescriptivism in his essay "The Prescriptive Tradition";

> In its most general sense, prescriptivism is the view that one variety of language has an inherently higher value than others, and that this ought to be imposed on the whole of the speech community. The view is propounded especially in relation to grammar and vocabulary, and frequently with reference to pronunciation.... Adherents to this variety are said to speak or write "correctly"; deviations from it are said to be "incorrect." (In *Language Awareness*, edited by P. Escholy et al. [New York: St. Martin's Press, 2000], p. 116)

The belief that one variety ought to be imposed as determining correctness is the issue being challenged throughout this chapter. What is not being challenged is the notion that one variety of a language does in fact emerge as the linguistic/political victor—the "standard," as it were—over other forms of the language in question. This is not being challenged because there is no need to deny the fact that one variety of language "dominates" others, and in time receives legitimation and validation with the imprimatur of some ruling body of guardians of the language.

Here again, David Crystal is informative:

> Some countries have felt that the best way to look after a language is to place it in the care of an academy. In Italy, the Accademia della Crusca was founded as early as 1582, with the object of purifying the Italian language. In France, in 1635, Cardinal Richelieu established the

> Académie française, which set the pattern for many subsequent bodies. . . . The 40 academicians were drawn from the ranks of the church, nobility, and the military— a bias which continues to the present day. (Ibid., p. 118)

That there are institutions, ideological mechanisms, that exist to help codify a language and help regulate usage is not in and of itself problematic; in fact, at times they are necessary. That many of these official and unofficial institutions often wield their power with dictatorial aplomb is the problem. The fact that the history of these institutions is a story of control and enforcement, of privilege and disadvantage, is what is wrong. What makes matters worse, of course, is that many who are in positions to help students advance their academic standing often accept the rigidity and narrow view from the top in the name of clarity.

In the introduction to his *Literacies of Power: What Americians Are Not Allowed to Know*, Donaldo Macedo asserts

> For me, the mundane call for language simplicity and clarity represents yet another mechanism to dismiss the complexity of theoretical issues, particularly if these theoretical constructs interrogate the prevailing dominant ideology. It is for this very reason that Gayatri Spivak correctly pointed out that the call for "plain prose cheats." I would go a step further and say: The call for plain prose not only cheats, it also bleaches. (p. 8)

Macedo quickly, and rightly, moves from these mechanisms to the bleaching of America. The various forces at work attempting to control and direct the standard language are whitewashing it, along with our culture, which demands more flexibilty, more mobility, and more acknowledgment of its diversity.

Some may feel that we may never get from underneath the weight of those pressing standard English down upon us. But, as I've been suggesting, if we push ourselves to get beyond the morality of speaking right, the possibilities are great. We must get beyond the rigidity of prescriptivism while respecting the history of our language, and the need to have a standard form of it to ensure the progress of our democracy. This is not a contradictory position; it is possible to conceive of a less rigidly defined and regulated standard while acknowledging the value and usefulness of such a standard.

As Molefi Kete Asante states in "An Afrocentric Communication Theory," from his book titled *Malcom X as Culture Hero and Other Afrocentric Essays,*

> I am concerned with nothing less than human maturity. It is my intention to address in a systematic way the pragmatics of communication, particularly with respect to the way we are affected by our environment. Such a task undertakes a reorientation of the enterprise of social science, a reformulation of assumptions, and a more thorough response to the diversity of human experience in communication. (p. 171)

The project of articulating a pragmatics of communication predicated on the diversity of human experience is, perhaps, the very project we must undertake to make progress with respect to getting beyond the morality of speaking right. It is the very acceptance of the shift from dogmatic enforcement to open agreement that leads the way.

One example of the consequences of such a shift is the move toward greater flexibility concerning the issue of "correctness." The strict prescriptivist's view would be that rules determine correctness. Many have come to see that often it is use that determines correctness. (This can be seen in operation regarding the shifts in spelling, possessives, etc., in the past three hundred years.) This view is often taken as a more flexible and liberal understanding of the notion of correctness. I am recommending that we take it one step further—that is, that use determines use. *That's it!* If a given community of speakers uses a word, phrase, pronunciation, spelling, or syntax, then it determines nothing more linguistically than use, a preference, a discursive habit. But correctness in this context is extra—that is, metalinguistic. This is so because the notion of correctness is something imposed after the linguistic fact. There is nothing inherently wrong with the desire to authorize a given use with the status of general acceptability (correctness), but how we get there is and has been the trick.

If more teachers understood and accepted this concept, then the teaching of standard English would automatically shift from the instruction and enforcement of rules of incontrovertible propriety to an engagement with students concerning, as Asante puts it, the pragmatics of communication. With such a shift would also come a shift in the presumption of the linguistic and moral superiority of standard English over and above nonstandard forms of the language. Teaching standard English could no longer rely on the false (absurd, according to Bill Bryson) claim that there exists some intrinsic value to this "variety" over others. No longer could a teacher count on the plea to preserve the tongue that Shakespeare spoke. That tongue is gone—whether for better or for worse, linguists and professors of English may debate. But from a pragmatics of communication, from a pragmatics of speaking English, it is simply the case that only Americans with aspirations for the theater speak that tongue. This does not, and ought not, in any way, devalue the significance of that older variety of English. Shakespeare, I am confident, will continue to garner the attention he deserves from all corners of the world. What it ought to emphasize is the dynamics of the English language and its ability (as is true for many languages) to continue to evolve, including new words, styles, and pronunciations.

Some might prefer that the standard English we speak be considered frozen, not capable of and not needing to change—existing, as it were, in a linguistic and cultural vacuum. But obviously this flies in the face of the changes in English since the time the British gained control of North America. Many of us may speak in ways not that unlike certain speakers from England, but it is clear our spelling, pronunciation, and use have been transformed over time and distance, sometimes more radically than not. Abandoning the notion that rules determine correctness and accepting the notion that use determines only use does not mean there is no need for rules; to the contrary, such a shift demands that rules play an essential role in the pragmatics of communication. It is the process of establishing them, accepting them, and teaching them that now comes under reconsideration.

That a majority of the literate people in the United States do read, write and speak standard English, to greater and lesser degrees of fluency, is a linguistic and political fact, the significance of which cannot be denied. That still many others, however, speak nonstandard forms of English, preeminent among them Black English, as well as other languages, such as Spanish, also should not be ignored. We must get beyond viewing nonstandard English and/or other languages as *ipso facto* some kind of "handicap," putting our nation's ability to communicate in jeopardy. The diversity of human experience, as Asante argues, must be incorporated into the pragmatics of communication, not obliterated or bleached out.

In her important book *Affirming Diversity: The Sociopolitical Context of Multicultural Education*, Sonia Nieto tells us:

Language diversity needs to be placed within a sociopolitical context to understand why speaking a language
other than English is not itself a handicap. On the
contrary, it can be a great asset to learning. . . . The
general view is that for dominated groups, bilingualism is
a burden; yet among middle-class and wealthy students,
it is an asset. It is not unusal to find in the same high
school the seemingly incongruous situation of one group
of students having their native language wiped out while
another group of students struggles to learn a foreign
language in a contrived and artificial setting. (p. 188)

The apparent double standard or blatant contradiction of the
attitude toward certain types of bilingualism speaks for itself.
The fact that more and more corporations doing business in
the "age of globalization" are placing a premium on new hires
who can read, write, and speak more than just English points
to utilitarian and corporate valuation of languages, including
Black English, to sell to hip-hop consumers, among others.
(One can almost imagine a corporate advertising meeting with
"translators" and "interpreters" of hip hop working as consul-
tants for McDonald's, the Gap, and Sony.) The business
"community" understands the value of the languages of all
other communities, as long as it sells.

Perhaps the resistance to acknowledging the linguistic and
historical value of Black English and the growing antagonism
toward Spanish is based on the belief that, if left unchecked,
the qualitiy of our nation (our democracy) will be under-
mined. All standards will be abandoned if we fail to maintain
the quality of our language, so the argument goes. But if, as I
have argued throughout this chapter, we view standard
English with the historical and linguistic respect it deserves,
we actually gain greater freedom to welcome additional
voices, with their lingustic alterations and contributions. This

is happening anyway. The point is to stop viewing it as an invasion, an attack upon our language and our nation. This is not 1066, the Norman Conquest is over, and the political and linguistic ramifications of that battle have made their permanent imprint on our language. Something different is taking place: an integration, not an invasion.

The Afro-American language that Baldwin and Baraka talk about is American, and we as a nation can no longer claim it to be substandard and can no longer be afraid of it infecting and undoing standard English. Standard English has demonstrated over the course of its dynamic history that it is as strong as it is pliable. We need to begin thinking of ways to get speakers of nonstandard English to see the benefits of gaining competency in standard English without negating their nonstandard form of the language. What can happen—what, in my opinion, should happen—is the continuation of the natural life of a language in a democratic society where a multitude of people influence the standard language.

This, of course, does not mean that anything goes at any time, but rather that the standard language is understood as something fluid (obviously less so than the trendy slang of teenagers and artists), but capable of incorporating new vocabulary and even syntax from diverse sources. This might one day mean that standard English officially acknowledges words, phrases, spellings, etc., that it does not now (i.e., that those in control do not yet accept). Even the French, try as they might with their powerful Académie française, cannot keep out foreign words and phrases, especially those from the United States. We are a far more diverse nation, one that has many influences and that will continue to have many influences. That some traditions should be safeguarded is without question, but to safeguard without questioning is obviously wrong. Too many traditions have proven themselves to be unfair, undemocratic.

There is more to consider, but this much seems clear: The teaching of standard English must be approached from within the linguistic, political, and historical context that produced the language and made it of value to our democracy today; and that the attitude toward nonstandard forms of the language, especially Black English, that they are "substandard," is linguistically and historically wrongheaded. Black English was begotten from a violent origin, and has been and remains an important (necessary?) part of African-American culture and therefore American culture. In what way it remains is perhaps part of the project of the pragmatics of communication that our nation needs to consider.

Every time I hear a teacher correct a student and then go on to misuse the pronoun "who" when "whom" should have been used, or when someone arguing for the need for rigorous enforcement of the rules of standard English mistakingly, but quite confidently, uses "I" instead of "me," because they are overcorrecting themselves (hypercorrection), I cannot help but wonder why there is all the resistence to reconsidering what the standard really is, but then I remember. It has little to do with language itself and everything to do with the morality of speaking right.

4.

Go Tell It on the Mount

Give me a place to stand, and I will move the world.

—Archimedes

I got the Holy Spirit
To help me run this race.
I got the Holy Spirit
It appointed my soul a place.

—James Baldwin, *The Amen Corner*

In his phenomenological study *Getting Back into Place*, philosopher Edward S. Casey tells us, "[w]here we are has a great deal to do with who and what we are." (p. 307) Where we are, where we come from, and where we go are all tied together, not always in simple and easily comprehensible ways but bound together nevertheless. We move foward and back, to and from places. We are drawn to places by their history, by what they represent and what they might come to be in the future. We take from and give to places; we are changed by, and sometimes make a difference at, the places we inhabit or visit. But finding a place, the right place, from which we can build, create, work, and thrive is perhaps the most important moment of "placing oneself" in the world. Simply put, where you have been, where you are, and where you will be matter.

The story of my coming to the College of Mount Saint Vincent is a story very much about finding a place, a place to stand and to take a stand. During my eight years as director of the Graduate Program in Urban and Multicultural Education, I have come to appreciate just how important a place Mount Saint Vincent has been, is, and will continue to be. This is so, in large part, due to the work and spirit of the Sisters of Charity, their ongoing commitment to social justice and serving those in need. That someone like me found his way to the college and the sisters is still cause for a mixture of amusement and some measure of disbelief among friends and colleagues alike. Yet it has been at the college, as director of the graduate program, that I have found a place to do the work that means so much to me and has come to matter to others. The story is important because it is the story about how this small institution gave me the opportunity to offer something of value to teachers: a program of graduate study far more engaging, dynamic, and caring than can be found at many other renowned schools of education. This is not to say that this is a story without its share of setbacks and failures, but it is ultimately a story about a *place* of possibility and transformation, capable of making a difference in the lives of teachers.

In the late spring of 1994 I decided to take a professional risk by changing jobs. Since 1990 I had been the director of the college preparatory programs in the School of Education at Queens College (CUNY). Among other duties, the directorship came with the responsibility of being the official liaison between Townsend Harris High School and the college. This is the position that first gave me the opportunity to work directly with teachers, allowing me to gain valuable insight into some of the complex issues that often frame, if not define, teaching at an urban public school.

Townsend Harris, it must be noted, is by no means a typical New York City public high school. Unlike the overwhelming majority of public schools (elementary, middle school, and other high schools), Townsend Harris was from the very start a fortunate place. The current Townsend Harris is a re-creation of the famed high school that was housed at City College of New York until 1942 and from which it derives its name. After many years and much political maneuvering by a very active and powerful alumni, the namesake was reborn at Queens College.

The original Townsend Harris High School was an all-male school that had an accelerated and rigorous curriculum grounded in Greek and Latin. After studying for three years, students became freshmen at City College. The graduates from Townsend Harris, and later City College, are among some of the most famous alumni of New York City public education, including the discoverer of the vaccine for polio, Jonas Salk. It was the strong desire of the alumni of this storied school that provided the vision for and force behind the new Townsend Harris High School, a Townsend Harris steeped in tradition but now enthusiastically welcoming female students and committed to serving the diverse population of New York City.

Since its rebirth in 1986, the high school had been temporarily housed a few blocks from the campus in a defunct yeshiva. The official opening of the new and permanent home of Townsend Harris at Queens College was set for the fall of 1994. My resignation, effective July 1, guaranteed that I would not, in any official capacity, be part of the exciting next phase of reincarnation of this special place.

There was much about my position at Queens College that made leaving difficult. In addition to working at a place that represented an important social commitment to education, I was graduated from the college's Philosophy Department, and studied art history and psychology there as well. I knew a great many like-minded people and had the opportunity to make new and lifelong friends. As a result, I continued to learn in new and different ways. (Some examples of this include my participation in the Monday lunch gatherings organized by the late Democratic-Socialist Michael Harrington, where political debates concerning current issues were always heated; my rigorous introduction to queer theory thanks to the ever-generous Steve Kruger; and my exposure to the compassionate pursuit of making educational institutions places of social conscience due to the tireless work of Barbara Bowen and Anthony O'Brien.) I was also fortunate enough, for the only time in my academic career so far, to have the staff and resources appropriate for the job I was hired to do. There was much to hold on to, especially if professional as well as emotional comforts were high priorities. It was not, therefore, an easy decision to leave friends and colleagues. I imagine that leaving such places should never be simple.

But despite all this, something inside me stirred and longed to move on. I was eager to work with teachers in a novel way that, unfortunately, could not take place at Queens—at that time, anyway. So when a colleague approached me, partly in jest, suggesting he had an "idyllic little place" for me to go experiment and meld my work in cultural theory and education, I wasn't all that surprised to feel excited. He had given me an advertisement for the position of director of a new graduate program at the College of Mount Saint Vincent focusing on urban and multicultural education. As I stood still, seriously reading the advertisement, he amusingly announced that there and then I was being summoned, and I should "go tell it on the Mount."

I was immediately convinced that the curriculum offered through the Graduate Program in Urban and Multicultural Education sounded like the perfect vehicle for me to further develop my ideas about, strategies for, and commitment to working with urban schoolteachers. It was a curriculum that gave me hope concerning the possibility of forging a more meaningful relationship among contemporary cultural theory, education, and the pursuit of social justice. My resignation, then, was motivated by my desire to have a genuine opportunity to work with teachers examining their everyday (lived) experiences based on a rigorous but interdisciplinary approach that aimed to combine intellectual rigor, political sophistication, and social compassion. It was, remember, late spring and emotions can run strong. I was smitten with the idea of heading off to the Bronx and beginning a new and exciting relationship.

There were, however, a number of details that disrupted my reverie and gave me reason for pause. In addition to the difficulty, alluded to above, of leaving the comfort of a place that had given me so much, something equally, if not more, significant began to make itself manifest. I had grown up in New York, went to school in New York, and had worked in New York most of my life, and yet I had never heard of the College of Mount Saint Vincent. I knew virtually nothing about it other than the somewhat obvious fact that it was a Catholic institution. This last point could not be considered inconsequential, given my political position concerning a number of issues. The fact that I did not even have a job interview set up at that point did not lessen my suddenly feeling a bit ill at ease. I believe my reaction to be somewhat typical for someone in the process of thinking about a job possibility, of projecting and fantasizing all things good, bad, or otherwise in comparison to life as one knows it. And, as fortune would have it, I was granted an interview and offered the job; thus my projections and fantasies were ultimately not in vain, though perhaps a bit premature.

When I met with Roland Yoshida, dean of the School of Education at Queens College, and my boss at the time, to discuss my desire to go forward with the new job, he smiled and said he knew it was just a question of when, and not if, I would move on to some other place. He had given me much advice and support during my tenure as director of the college preparatory programs, permitting me to experiment in many ways. He was generous and encouraging, and he provided me with a model for administrating that is still very much part of my own approach today: he enabled people to do their work. We both enjoyed cooking and shared more than a few good meals together; he knew that his opinion meant a lot to me, so he was perhaps particularly careful of what he said. When our meeting was just about over, he cautioned me on two points. He predicted that I would be successful in making the best of the new program, "doing exactly what is needed to further the professional development of teachers from an urban and multicultural perspective." But he warned that I should be mindful of just how "charged and controversial such a perspective in education remained, especially in light of the blacklash to political correctness that is under way." He also warned me to be prepared to work to the point of exhaustion, "because that is how small colleges operate and survive." As he bluntly put it, "the more energy you have and the better you work, the more you will work. It's a given, a formula for success, but one that comes at an obvious price." He stood up, offered me his hand, and asked me to help him find my replacement. With that friendly yet official gesture, he said good-bye.

The College of Mount Saint Vincent was founded by the Sisters of Charity in 1910 and admitted only women (becoming coeducational in 1974). Originally founded in 1847 as the Academy of Mount Saint Vincent, it was located on a parcel of land known as McGown's Pass that is now part of the northern end of Central Park in Manhattan (at approximately Fifth Avenue and 109th Street). When New York City decided to create Central Park, the Sisters of Charity were forced to leave. The New York State Legislature authorized the city to take advantage of its power of eminent domain to seize all the land between Eighth Avenue and Fifth Avenue and from 110th Street to 59th Street (the current western, eastern, northern, and southern borders, respectively, of Central Park), and to evict the nearly two thousand people who established a network of shantytowns that many wealthy merchants living on Fifth Avenue wanted removed. Included among the residents living on this land were Irish and German immigrants working as pig farmers and gardeners, and the members of Seneca Village, an African-American settlement at 82nd Street and Eighth Avenue that had as many as three churches and a school. Along with these others, the Sisters of Charity were ousted and had to find a new place to call home.

By 1857, the Sisters of Charity purchased land in the Riverdale section of the Bronx. The College of Mount Saint Vincent now stands on land once owned by a renowned Shakespearean actor of his day, Edwin Forrest, who sold approximately fifty acres to the sisters for $100,000. His estate overlooked the Hudson River and had a number of buildings that could be utilized, including the landmark "Fonthill Castle." The campus today is more than seventy acres and slopes downhill from Riverdale Avenue to the Hudson River, bordering the city of Yonkers to the north and stretching down to 261st Street on its southern border. Among its other physical attributes, the campus has a lovely pond and many beautiful chestnut trees. The College of Mount Saint Vincent is an urban liberal arts college blessed with a pastoral campus.

My first visit to the College felt something like an excursion to the Hudson River Valley in upstate New York. I remember a high blue sky and bright sun. I was taken by the hilly contour of the campus, the rich green of its lawns and the spectacular view of the Hudson River and the Palisades cliffs of New Jersey. Upon entering the campus I experienced a tranquillity not commonly encountered in contemporary New York City. It seemed a somewhat anachronistic place, real but evoking another time. The mood of the campus was disconcerting—I had an image of a New York that long ago got filled in, flattened, paved over, and erased. That day the campus invited me to traverse a terrain that linked the past, present, and future. As I walked, I felt the spirit of the place, and with each step I felt emboldened. I was convinced that things could happen here, that I, to quote James Baldwin, had been "appointed" a place.

My appointment to the position of director of the graduate program came at a time of great change for Mount Saint Vincent as well as for me. Just one year prior to my appointment, the college named Mary C. Stuart the first layperson (and first non-Sister of Charity) as president. In addition, my program was only the second graduate program to be offered at the college, and there was, and remains, much concern about the impact of graduate studies on an institution committed to and identified with teaching undergraduates. These important developments, coupled with the fact that the new population of undergraduate students represented a racial and economic shift from the historically Irish-American and Italian-American alumnae, only added to the dramatic sense of change at the college—Mount Saint Vincent was transforming itself into a genuinely diversified institution of higher education, culturally and programmatically.

Mount Saint Vincent had remained a small and predominantly white female college in the Catholic tradition until the late 1980s and early 1990s. Contemporaneous with my arrival, Mount Saint Vincent found itself growing in the number of traditionally underrepresented enrollments, becoming an institution with a large Hispanic, African-American, and Asian-American student body rapidly outnumbering the traditional white ethnic population. It was an institution also in the midst of developing and expanding its graduate programs. Needless to say, Mount Saint Vincent was neither fully prepared for nor properly equipped to meet all the challenges that come with sudden change. Yet despite the confusion and frustration of some and the resistance of others, the Mount Saint Vincent faculty and staff, in partnership with the Sisters of Charity, moved ahead.

Oddly enough, when I arrived in late August 1994 there were only seven students enrolled in the graduate program, and just two courses were offered that first semester. I was daunted by the lack of students, the high expectations to successfully recruit more students, and the need to make the program financially sound. Nevertheless, encountering the powerful dialogue and critical analysis emanating from those in the program that inaugural semester, I was even more convinced of the significance of the curriculum and its potential to assist teachers. The question before me was: Is there a way to let people know about this place?

Sure in my conviction that something special was under way at Mount Saint Vincent, I decided to roll the dice and embark on an all-out recruitment strategy. My timing—on the surface, anyway—could not have been worse: New York City was still smarting from the turmoil of the "Rainbow Curriculum," which culminated in the resignation of Joseph Fernandez, the city's schools chancellor. Among other controversial issues, Fernandez's advocacy of the multiculturally based Rainbow Curriculum proved too much for some local school districts and their very vocal board members, and drew considerable negative attention nationally for the inclusion of a book titled *Heather Has Two Mommies*. Meanwhile, the neighboring city of Yonkers was embroiled in a bitter series of lawsuits and public debates over the segregation of its housing and schools, which were tearing that city apart. Add to all of this the overall mood of New York after a racially charged election in which Rudolph Giuliani defeated David Dinkins, the first black mayor of New York, and it is pretty clear that leaving the campus of Mount Saint Vincent to sing the praises of a new graduate program in urban and multicultural education was, to put it tactfully if somewhat immodestly, daring.

In some real sense, fortunately, my timing could not have been better. Although tensions ran high in all quarters, it was still clear to almost everybody involved, perhaps even more so than ever before, that teachers and administrators needed to critically and rigorously reconsider their strategies and practice, to have an honest dialogue about urban teaching and multiculturalism. What made the program offered through Mount Saint Vincent palatable to so many different people was, in large part, the *place* itself. Unlike many other colleges and universities in New York City, Mount Saint Vincent was not perceived, and rightly so, as being ideologically dogmatic. There was something nonthreatening to those who considered the program simply because Mount Saint Vincent was far from the center of any public controversy. Mount Saint Vincent, for example, has neither a Leonard Jefferies, whose strong and animated positions concerning Afrocentricism has made him infamous and has caused City College of New York its share of grief, nor a Diane Ravitch, whose work as assistant secretary of education, under the forceful and conservative direction of William Bennett during the Reagan/Bush era, still makes her suspect for many progressive educators and thus a problematic, albeit well-known figure for New York University. Mount Saint Vincent was, on the other hand, simply too small to be considered a place attempting to strong-arm anyone. Its lack of prestige and notoriety made it possible for people to consider the program without the typical political concerns and baggage: After all, what threat could a group of nuns or their emissaries represent?

Interestingly, in 1994 there were no other registered programs in New York State designed specifically to address urban and multicultural education. True, there were a number of programs, at both the masters and doctoral levels, that had courses on multicultural and urban educational issues, but there were no programs dedicated to urban and multicultural education leading to a degree. The combination of these circumstances—the uniqueness of the curriculum; the fact that the program was housed at a college that posed no ostensible threat by either institutional reputation or individual personality; and the consensus, even if tacit and tentative, among educational leaders that a multicultural perspective of some kind was needed to improve teaching and learning—gave me the opportunity to "go tell it on the Mount."

Everywhere I went I was cordially greeted, even by traditional adversaries and critics of multiculturalism. Part of the reason for this was noted above, but another important factor was my ability to link educational success, social justice, and democratic spirit to the mission and values of Mount Saint Vincent. The college's historical commitment to advocating a "values-centered" curriculum made it easier for me to present the graduate program as a natural extension of the ethical values and vision of the Sisters of Charity and the faculty. This meant that whatever preconceived notions and antagonism my audiences might have had were challenged and ameliorated by virture of "the place I was coming from." People from many different agencies, schools, and religious affiliations heard the spirit of the message and felt open to, if not totally comfortable with, the words of criticism and demands for change that guide the curriculum and pedagogical strategies of the program.

For the first time, many began to understand that not everyone involved with challenging the prejudiuce and injustice infused into school curricula across the nation was engaged in waging a culture war. Their fears of simply being labeled, and summarily dismissed as, racists, sexists, class elit-ists, agists, homophobics, etc., were assuaged by a call to meet the *needs* of children and the teachers who work with them every day in a new spirit. This meant confronting the vast and intimidating realities created by racism, homophobia, sexism, class elitism, agism, and discriminatory attitudes toward those with physical challenges from a place where one could feel safe to address such issues in the world and within oneself. The curriculum, the college, and the spirit of the Sisters of Charity and the faculty teaching in the program all helped create such a place.

From such a place no task could be viewed as beyond reach, too grand or immense. As the French philosopher Gaston Bachelard eloquently wrote in *The Poetics of Space*:

> When a relaxed spirit meditates and dreams, immensity seems to expect images of immensity. The mind sees and continues to see objects, while the spirit finds the nest of immensity in an object. We shall have various proofs of this if we follow the daydreams that the single word vast inspired in Baudelaire. Indeed, vast is one of the most Bauldelairian of words, the word that marks most natu-rally, for this poet, infinity of intimate space. (p. 190)

From the intimate space of Mount Saint Vincent, the vast project of pursuing social justice in schools, of pursuing educational success began to take form. Just what form this project took, I do not believe anyone could have predicted.

My first year at Mount Saint Vincent had proved my old boss's words true. As dean Roland Yoshida had warned, I was exhausted. That first year I went to, presented at, and met with anyone or any group willing to talk with me about urban education, multiculturalism, and the program. Though I was fatigued, I was excited because things were truly starting to happen. Little did I realize at the time, however, that my last meeting of the academic year 1994–95 would prove to redefine, for me, the meaning of the phrase "make things happen."

As I have been claiming throughout this chapter, "place" is profoundly important. This is even more so once we acknowledge both the multiplicity and complexity of place—that is to say, when we fully begin to understand "places." There is no place if in fact there is not some other place from which to discern one's own position, one's status in the world. For us to have a genuine sense and appreciation of the place where we reside, where we are, we must have some sense of where we are not. The logic here demands that *this* place does not exist *if there is no other* place. Our knowledge of place, therefore, is contingent on the possibility of there being other places, even if our awareness of them is vague and incomplete. My awareness of where I was became all the more intensified upon encountering a place greatly different from Mount Saint Vincent, a place that was to become my other place.

My last scheduled meeting for the year was with Barbara Tubertini, the coordinator of inservice and graduate courses for the New York City Teacher Center (the professional development division of the United Federation of Teachers). Unlike my first encounter with Mount Saint Vincent, which instilled a sense of calm, the Teacher Center was a place of pure motion, of tight spaces filled with energetic people moving at top speed. Whereas Mount Saint Vincent evoked a pastoral setting, entering the Teacher Center felt like entering the New York Stock Exchange, where not a single moment or gesture was wasted. The fact that the Teacher Center is housed at the headquarters of the United Federation of Teachers (the New York City teachers' union) and located on Park Avenue South and Twenty-First Street, one of the busiest areas of Manhattan these days, only adds to the frenetic sensation one gets upon entering the world of the Teacher Center.

The meeting with Barbara Tubertini was scheduled for late in the day and was to be a short information exchange about the needs and desires of the Teacher Center, constituency, and what, if anything, the Graduate Program in Urban and Multicultural Education might offer to serve those needs and desires. Within minutes it was clear that I was being given a special opportunity. I had come prepared to speak in general terms about the value of the program and why teachers might benefit from participating in a program with our particular focus. Barbara Tubertini quickly pushed me to elaborate further about the nature of the program and to explain how it was different from other programs offering courses on multiculturalism and urban education; she wanted to know everything about the program.

She and I talked about many things, including teachers' apprehension concerning the polarizing impact of addressing racism in the classroom and the curriculum. When we finally paused for a coffee break we realized that we had been talking for approximately two and a half hours straight and that her staff and colleagues had already gone home. Given that there was still much more to discuss, we decided to call it a day and made plans to continue the conversation the next day. As we said good night, Barbara told me to come prepared to work out something concrete: she wanted to include my program in her offerings to teachers, and she wanted to get it going quickly. While walking home, it dawned on me that she was giving me the chance to offer my program through a collaboration with the Teacher Center, a partnership that would guarantee the successful dissemination of a curriculum and perspective that I knew would be of value to new and experienced teachers alike.

That night I walked from my home on Eighteenth Street down to Battery Park thinking over everything we had discussed and what I could present to Barbara by the next day. I walked along West Street, staring out over the Hudson

River toward New Jersey and was mindful of the difference between my view of the river from Mount Saint Vincent and this particular setting. From Mount Saint Vincent, New Jersey is bucolic, just trees, the red-brown rockface of the Palisades cliffs, and no buildings to be seen anywhere. The view from lower Manhattan is a stark contrast. Looking south and west, one can see only a spectacularly well-defined urban landscape. Farther downtown ahead of me, the twin towers of the World Trade Center and westward the port of Bayonne, Jersey City, and Hoboken dynamically replaced the red-brown Palisades cliffs. The same Hudson River divided New York and New Jersey, but the emotions and energy carried along its currents seemed transformed. The calm from Mount Saint Vincent fed directly into the hectic and ever-widening river of millions of commuters, workers, and inhabitants, all flowing at the accelerated speed demanded by this realm of city life. It was while gazing into this electrified nighttime view of urban vastness that I began to see what might be possible.

That next day was charged; I was excited and felt that the end of the academic year actually punctuated the beginning of my work. Barbara and I picked up right where we had left off the day before. She told me that she, too, felt much was possible but had spent part of the previous night wondering whether I was a mere professorial illusion that would disappear the moment the work got under way. I told her of my own musings from the same night. We laughed at each other's fantasies. I reassured her that I was for real and would not suddenly go away like some kind of academic apparition, like many professors evidently have done in the past. She in turn reminded me that we were attempting to deal with a relatively small portion of the vastness I gazed into the other night and that, however evocative, we might do well to simply begin by looking at some of the specifics of our collaboration and save the gazing for another time.

We both realized that each of us was committed and that the places we come from, though obviously different, were complementary to each other in many ways. That day, Barbara and I navigated the powerful river that connects these two places and charted a course that would make a lasting difference. Although other universities and colleges offered courses, and even entire master's programs, through the Teacher Center, Barbara and I embarked on a genuinely collaborative journey, a mutually engaged partnership that would allow all involved to take a pedagogically pragmatic, ethically grounded, and theoretically sophisticated voyage to some other place. That day we knew we were heading to places unknown.

Some readers anxious to get more of the details concerning courses, setting up the off-campus master's program, and the like will most likely be somewhat disappointed. My goal, after all, is not to document or catalog these things as such, important as they are. Instead, my purpose is to give voice to and emphasize the equally important and sadly too often overlooked significance of the fact that, to quote Edward S. Casey again, "where we are has a great deal to do with who and what we are."

Barbara Tubertini and I are very much the people we are, in large part because of where we are. This is by no means to claim that who and what we are should be understood as our being only "products" or "by-products" of the places we currently inhabit. I have earlier suggested than this would be too simple, that things are more complex than this, that Casey's statement involves our past and future as well as our present places. Like so many others, instead of being merely "determined" by the places and circumstances in which we find ourselves, Barbara and I are examples of people responding to and being affected by places in profound ways. Had I gone to some place other than Mount Saint Vincent or decided to remain at Queens College, I most likely would not have been in a position to meet Barbara (or if I did, would not be able to offer her the program and spirit of Mount Saint Vincent). Similarly, if Barbara simply had been somewhere else in the vast system of New York City public education, even somewhere other within the Teacher Center, chances are that she would not be involved in meeting people like me, and developing courses and programs that have come to be so important for literally thousands of New York City teachers. Her legacy would no doubt still be of value, but it would radically differ from the one she will leave now because of the place she did inhabit.

The value of discussing and describing courses and programs in detail (in the manner that is familiar to and typically demanded by academic researchers and policy analysts) cannot be denied. Unfortunately, too many times the value of the individuals, the places, and the spirit that make the courses and programs come alive and matter, get relegated to a far more subordinate realm of consideration and worth, if not ignored altogether. In some ways this makes sense; people do need to know the nuts and bolts of a successful course or program to understand them and perhaps to replicate or adapt them in some fashion, as well as to assess them, of course. But what usually gets short shrift and devalued as mere fuzzy, nonempirical "process" stuff are the people, how they teach, administer, and communicate, and the spirit of the specific places where all these things successfully happen.

In discussing the relationships between some specific universities and community partnerships, David J. Maurrasse astutely notes the importance of the spirit, mission, and culture of a place (university or college). In his book *Beyond the Campus: How Colleges and Universities Form Partnerships with Their Communities*, he tells us

> I am thinking of mission [spirit and culture] more in terms of a "way of doing business," in addition to a "reason for being." In some cases, institutions of higher

education may be suited to partnering with local communities rhetorically, but various aspects of their structure and culture may hinder healthy community partnerships. (p. 7)

Too frequently, the "way of doing business" is reduced to those quantifiable things we are offered as evidence for this or that, and what gets lost in the accounting of these things is the tenor and mood of the people and places involved.

My point is straightforward and simple: great books, great curriculums and syllabi do not and cannot automatically add up to great courses, programs, and interactions (a lesson, Maurrasse suggests, many universities and school systems seem never to learn). Too many great books have been badly discussed and analyzed by too many indifferent and hostile professors and teachers. And too many good professors, teachers, and students have found themselves, time and time again, overwhelmed by the politics, mood, and culture of the very place where teaching and learning are supposed to occur. Relationships between people and places need to be more fully acknowledged and explored in the fashion suggested here, at least more so than is usually the case. Such relationships are, in my opinion, as important as, if not more important than, the "nuts and bolts" empirical stuff that many people seem to count on.

Politically, culturally, and institutionally, for example, it might at first appear that the publically funded and secular Teacher Center and the privately financed and religion-based College of Mount Saint Vincent are places worlds apart, with little in common. But because each place shares a "way of doing business," they are able work together. Each, with its own tradition, is and has been committed to serving others through education; each has attracted and welcomed people like Barbara and me, among other kindred spirits. These are places that have given us a chance to pursue our vision of things and to go beyond the boundaries we encounter. As a result, something special has happened to us and the places where we work—in this case, not just the distribution of some courses off-campus but also the meaningful dissemination of a curriculum honed and further developed together in collaboration because of the establishment of the partnership that allowed such a collaboration to occur.

Barbara and I established trust and respect. That each of us could be worthy of trust and respect is, arguably, the result of many factors, simple and complex. Both of us, however, come from places that allow people like us, intentionally and not, to do what we need and want to do. Each place, in its own unique way, is a place of commitment and service. Because of this, we have been able to go somewhere else together—a third place, if you like, a place characterized by partnership and collaboration.

In the time we have created and occupied this new place, we and our colleagues have grown intellectually and professionally in ways that would not have been possible had we started from some different place. Where we have been, where we are, and where we will be, matter. Together we have organized a successful annual conference, published a jointly produced series titled "Dialogue with Teachers," and developed a meaningful and rigorous off-campus master's program focusing on urban and multicultural education that ultilizes "distinguished practitioners" from the very schools and districts that our graduate students (themselves teachers) come from, among other accomplishments.

All of these achievements are important, in part because of how they came about—"where they came from," so to speak. The "way of doing business," the nonquantifiable, fuzzy process stuff, really does matter. It matters, for example, that both the Teacher Center and Mount Saint Vincent communicate as equal partners and value each other's commitment to service. Because of the new place we have created together, we have altered, however modestly—however locally, as it were—the way in which people from colleges and universities work with teachers and school personnel. By establishing a place of collegial respect, by being engaged in an authentic partnership, teachers and staff developers are expecting and now requesting a new "way of doing business" with professors and institutions of higher education.

Needless to say, much more needs to be done to further improve the quality of teacher education and the nature of university-school interactions. In my opinion, however, something necessary, if not quite sufficient, has already taken place. The spirit of cooperation, partnership and collaboration that emanates from the diverse but complementary places where Barbara, I, and our colleagues come from allows us all to go to still some other place together. The power of Mount Saint Vincent, for me, is its rich history of commitment to service, that it is precisely the sort of place it has been, is, and will continue to be. It is a place that has a history, a spirit, and a vision of what is possible. It is a place from which you naturally bring that history, spirit, and vision with you wherever you go.

At the end of her novel *Breath, Eyes and Memory*, Edwidge Danticat evocatively writes, "I come from a place where breath, eyes and memory are one, a place from which you carry your past like the hair on your head" (p. 234). I, too, come from such a place.

5.

But Is He Straight?

Identity, Teaching, and the Simple Acts of Privilege

I vividly remember the collective expression of dismay and disbelief coming from the students in my Philosophy 101 class after I got married. Upon my entering the classroom, it seemed as if everyone, at exactly the same moment, noticed that I was wearing a wedding ring. What struck me as particularly odd at the time were the ensuing comments concerning my sexuality and the fixity of my identity. "I told you he was straight," said a young woman sitting in the front row. "That don't mean shit," forcefully responded her female campanion. "Don't forget that he puts nail polish on his toes," added an older male student, apparently to no one in particular. For a moment or two I was taken aback; it was the first time in a very long time that I found myself self-consciously in front of a class.

Part of my reaction was due to the frank and, to my mind, indiscreet comments made without any concern as to whether I could hear them. But part of my response was due to my on-the-spot retroactive awareness that my class obviously had strong opinions about my sexualtiy, about who and what I was. I felt more a sense of embarrassment that the class had such thoughts about me than annoyance with the fact that they willing to voice their uncensored opinions so vocally upon the slight provocation of the wearing of a wedding ring. Somehow the articulation of their "take" on me made me feel awkward and uneasy in a way I had, up to that point, never encountered in academia. Although they were expressing themselves quite publicly, it was as if I were hearing their unconscious speak. The mixture of unsolicited and direct comments about my identity surprised and somewhat frightened me. At that moment, the protective armor of heterosexual privilege had been stripped from me, and I stood before the class confronted by the resulting naked truth.

I was *only* wearing a wedding ring. It belonged to my father-in-law and was given to me as a gift. I was experimenting with wearing it on and off the first few days since the marriage ceremony, trying to decide whether or not it was something I wanted to wear regularly. That I chose to wear the ring to class was of little significance, or so I thought. As it turned out, my simple and relatively meaningless gesture proved to be a significant act for my students and consequently an important one for me as well. Suddenly, and rather unceremoniously, I realized that my students were confused by how I presented myself, by how I represented myself. They were now perplexed and trying figure out whether I was "straight."

Such confusion, as Judith Butler notes in her groundbreaking *Gender Trouble*, may be due in part because

> gender is not always constituted coherently or consistently in different historical contexts, and because gender intersects with racial, class, ethnic, sexual, and regional modalities of discursively constituted identities. As a result, it becomes impossible to separate out "gender" from the political and cultural intersections in which it is invariably produced and maintained. (p. 3)

Whatever the "discursively constituted identities" of my students or me were at that particular moment, their "confusion" apparently reached an unacceptable level, resulting in the

explosion of comments and responses to the "troubling" mod-
ifications caused by the wearing of the wedding ring. Understood as an explicitly fixed symbol, the wedding ring, for these
students, represented the epitome of a historically stabilized,
if not iconically frozen, identity. In their eyes, the wedding
ring represented an identity that could not tolerate or accept
the ambiguous, ambivalent, and fluid identity (gender blending, to use a phrase) that I had unwittingly expressed through
various "political" and "cultural" acts (i.e., what I spoke about
and how I spoke about it, how I dressed, acted, and so on).
Their reactions were, in part, understandable rejections of
those political and cultural intersections, of what was for them
the incompatible intersections of heterosexual and queer
identities.

As I said, I was simply *wearing* a wedding ring. Yet, as
Butler persuasively argues:

> There is no gender identity behind the expressions of
> gender; that identity is performatively constituted by the
> very "expressions" that are said to be its results. (Ibid.,
> p. 25)

Thus my wearing of the wedding ring was one act among
many that, according to Butler, contribute to the performatively constituted identity that such gestures—expressions, as
she puts it—bring into existence. In this formulation, Butler,
following Nietzsche's lead, claims that such expressions (acts
and gestures) are not merely signposts pointing to some
substance or being "behind" the performative act. Instead, she
wants us to see that we ought to acknowledge the validity of
Nietzsche's bold assertion from *On the Genealogy of Morals* that
"there is no 'being' behind doing, effecting, becoming; the
doer is merely a fiction added to the deed . . . the deed is everything" (p. 45). Even if one is still tempted to remain committed

to someone "behind" the deed, Butler forces the issue: identity is as much a question of performance as it is one of metaphysical inheritance. In other words, given the full complexity of the "racial, class, ethnic, sexual, and regional modalities of discursively constituted identities," there are no such things as "simple" acts, gestures, or expressions. It is within this context—that is, a complicated performative context—that I want to discuss identity, teaching, and privilege.

For many schoolteachers and college professors of different political leanings, there is a strong desire to maintain the myth of the "simple act"—an act, as they see it, free from the complicated modalities of discursively constituted identities. This desire finds expression in different ways and in varying degrees of contradiction, indifference, and outright absurdity. One useful example that comes to mind is the story told by Harvard Law School professor Lani Guinier (presented as one segment of the video "Democracy in a Different Voice" by Media Education Foundation). Professor Guinier recounts the experience she had in her business law class while a law student at Yale University. As she movingly tells the story, her law professor, upon entering the lecture hall for the first time that semester, gazed out over the class and greeted the entire class, both men and women alike, with the salutation he had used during his long career at Yale Law School. "Good morning, gentlemen," her professor welcomingly announced. The professor immediately went on to acknowledge the presence of women in the lecture hall, but apologetically asserted that he would continue to address everyone in attendance that day and thereafter "simply" as gentlemen, for, as he put it, it was his habit. He went further to explain that he certainly meant no disrespect; in fact, as he saw it, it was a gesture toward equality: all attending his lecture were, according to his rationale (and habit), to be described as "gentlemen," equally and without prejudice concerning one's actual gender. With this explanation, he went on simply as usual, business class as usual. With this explanation we have yet another justification and vindication of a "simple act."

Another example that sheds some light on the issue of simple acts is the somewhat bizarre incident involving a nun who teaches at an elite Catholic school on the upper East Side of Manhattan and one of her second graders. The story was covered by *New York Daily News* staff writer Michele McPhee. It went to press with the headline "Nun in Racial Flap" (*Daily News*, September 15, 2000). As McPhee reports it, the student, Kingsley Braggs, age seven,

> came home from St. Ignatius Loyola grammar school this week and asked his mother to cut his curly [nappy?] hair and shave his arms.
>
> When she asked why, the little boy showed her a worksheet on which his teacher, Sister Mary Seton, had scrawled "like a monkey!" under the word "handsome," which he had written to describe himself. (p. 6)

Commenting on the incident, the Reverend Walter Modrys, pastor of the school's parish, "insisted the nun wrote the words as a 'term of endearment'" (Ibid., 6). Continuing with his argument and defense of Sister Mary Seton's comment, the pastor protested that it was not fair to characterize the nun's words as racist or intentionally harmful to the young child.

> I don't think it's fair to take this remark totally out of context and imagine that the teacher is standing with the Ku Klux Klan hurling racist remarks at children.... It was meant in a very affectionate way. (p. 6)

This gesture was intended as a simple act of affection. Sister Mary Seton, not unlike Lani Guinier's law professor, meant no disrespect to anyone. It was simply her way of expressing "affection."

Unfortunately, Sister Mary Seton's warm gaze and the law professor's habitual gaze of equality, both instances of simple acts of support and acceptance, had painful and complicated consequences because of the regional modalities Butler calls to our attention. Even as a sophisticated law student, Lani Guinier was troubled by the "welcome" that her law professor and Yale Law School offered to her. But little Kingsley Braggs was more than troubled by his teacher's comment; he wanted to immediately eradicate the problem, namely how the nun saw him, by altering how *he looked*. Sister Mary Seton's gaze redescribed what Kingsley Braggs had seen of himself, in himself: a "handsome" boy. The nun affectionately gazed upon her student and simply stated what she felt. The law professor welcomely gazed upon his class and simply stated what he felt. Two simple acts, two acts meant to bridge differences and express acceptance and support.

Years after her encounter, Professor Lani Guinier revisited the site of the welcoming gaze and stared back, back at the callousness, back at the absurdity of the simple gesture. She was able because of her years of experience and maturity to look back at her law professor and Yale Law School. Her agency, her "oppositional gaze," as bell hooks asserts, is predicated on her ability to think and see through the law professor's simple act of description and find the space to redescribe and reclaim her own identity. As bell hooks observes in her 1992 essay "The Oppositional Gaze,"

> [s]paces of agency exist for black people, wherein we can both interrogate the gaze of the Other but also look back, and at one another, naming what we see. The "gaze" has been and is a site of resistance for colonized black people globally. Subordinates in relations of power learn experientially that there is a critical gaze, one that "looks" to document, one that is oppositional. In resistance struggle, the power of the dominated to assert

agency by claiming and cultivating "awareness" politicizes "looking" relations—one learns to look a certain way in order to resist. (p. 116)

By "looking back" at her professor's simple gesture, Professor Guinier was able to confront and challenge the gaze that rendered her one of the white "gentlemen" in the class. Her ability to do so afforded her the chance to critically "interrogate" a simple act.

But Kingsley Braggs was just a second grader at the time of his encounter with Sister Mary Seton's simple act of affection. Lacking the sophistication of a law student (even a nervous one), this little boy, this seven-year-old child, did what most children do: he went home and told his mother to change things, to make him look right. In his attempt to have his hair cut, Kingsley Braggs inadvertently disrupted the simple act of affection of Sister Mary Seton. Her "affectionate" gaze, her act of "generosity," was challenged by the oppositional gaze of his mother. "There is no excuse," said Kingsley's mother, "in the year 2000 [for] someone to call an African-American child a monkey. It's unacceptable" (*New York Daily News*, September 15, 2000, p. 6).

By going home and requesting to have his hair cut and his arms shaved, Kingsley Braggs created the space, painful as it was for him and his family, to call attention to, if not to interrogate, the gaze of Sister Mary Seton. Regardless of her intent, her simple act of affection caused this seven-year-old boy to go home and attempt to modify his troubling identity, to perform the not-so-simple act of cutting his hair and shaving his arms. His act of agency was to go home and have his mother perform a corrective task. Fortunately for him, his act of resistance came via his mother's oppositional gaze. She was able to, as bell hooks notes, "look back," and to deflect the gaze of Sister Mary Seton, well-intentioned as it might have been.

Every day across America, in schools, universities, and professional settings, such simple acts occur. Typically, those who perform them, sometimes out of mere habit and sometimes as a specifically well-intentioned gesture, do not seek confrontation and mean no disrespect. They seek only consistency and coherency in the world *they* inhabit. Yet every day across America, such simple acts offend, hurt, and antagonize those who encounter and endure them. The response to my wearing of the wedding ring necessarily prompted a reconsideration of my simple act of privilege.

Those involved with teaching are often asked (more often required) to consider how they "perform" in the classroom. They are typically evaluated according to a somewhat formulaic, if not orthodox, procedure of observation. For schoolteachers over the past twenty years or so, though many people would deny it, they *must* follow their "well-conceived" lesson plan. Even though educational leaders, policymakers, and even politicians know and admit that there is much more to good teaching than following a lesson plan, the focus of the observation and evaluation is, almost always, an emphasis on "the plan." Sometimes there is consideration of performative dynamics, but this is usually little more than lip service to the much-tarnished process of teaching as such. The real focus of these discussions is classroom management, control, and students' performance on "reliable" outcome assessments rather than serious consideration of the performative aspects of teaching itself. As Kenneth J. Saltman notes in his book *Collateral Damage: Corporatizing Public Schools—A Threat to Democracy*:

> The emphasis on discipline includes tightened curricular guidelines, and more standardized curricula geared toward the reduction of teacher autonomy, teacher deskilling, and the elimination of teaching as an intellec-

tural endeavor. . . . For example, some critics [of public education] call for heightened top-down control in the form of the complete replacement of teacher-made lesson plans with prefabricated scripted lessons. (p. 81)

The push is for results, and talking about how one does what one does—in this case, teaching—gets little if any real attention. How one "performs" is really a matter of how one's students behave and "achieve."

At the college and university level, though many people would deny it, a version of the lesson plan also plays a large role in the evaluation of an instructor. Though certainly more subtly enforced, the process of evaluating an instructor typically focuses on a lesson plan of some sort. An observer usually zeros in on an instructor's "knowledge" of the subject and her or his ability to "clearly" present information to the class. As is the case with a schoolteacher following a plan, the college instructor is expected to "perform" according to established decorum and protocol. Of course, there is nothing inherently problematic about the requirement to be organized, clear, and informative; such a requirement is only fair. Unfortunately, the reliance on traditionally accepted modes of expression and style—that is, comformity to the college lesson plan—normally precludes any serious consideration of the performative elements that are in fact part of the classroom dynamics. There is rarely any space or time given to discussions about topics such as body movement, tone of voice, style of dress (including the wearing or not wearing of wedding rings), or the type of examples and analogies employed by the instructor. The presumption is that "knowledge" is all that really matters; how one performatively executes or dispatches information is of little significance, unless of course the observer is personally offended or otherwise moved to specifically react to some expression or deed occurring during the class. Then awkwardly and defensively, the instructor must first justify and then usually alter her or his performance or risk possible unwanted consequences when tenure or promotion is being considered.

In their collection of essays *I've Got a Story to Tell: Identity and Place in the Academy*, Sandra Jackson and Jose Solis Jordan bring together narratives that strive

> to further the discourse regarding the multiple interrelationships of identity, self, others, pedagogy and institutions of higher education. The accounts that follow describe what it means to be a professor within the contested terrain of higher education, to break silences, and to speak the unspeakable: the subjectivities of women and men of color as educators contending with issues of race, gender, and class in their personal and pedagogical practices. (p. 1)

These are the narratives that are traditionally left out of the observations and evaluations. These are the discursively constituted identities that must conform to "the plan" or risk institutional retribution. *I've Got a Story to Tell* breaks the silence and disrupts the plan. But such a volume only highlights that how one performs in the class and what one chooses as examples—whether golf, the stock market, buying property, getting married, or whatever normally does not matter if one gives into the canonical plan. There is no need, for the sake of a common evaluation, to push further and ask why one chose this example or that analogy, as long as the observer understands and agrees. There is no need to consider the all too often "unspeakable" dimensions of teaching, as long as one performs (conforms) according to plan—in other words, as long as the instructor *plays* it straight and white.

Whether it is a middle school teacher or a full professor teaching graduate students, little, if any, emphasis is genuinely placed on how one performs, especially the "simple acts." But if, following the implication of Butler's analysis, there are no simple acts, then it is necessary to reconsider how any teacher "acts" in the classroom. Such reconsideration must take place within the complicated historical context that Butler calls to our attention, the very performative context usually ignored or dismissed by those thinking about pedagogy.

The reason my "simple act" of wearing a wedding ring was problematic needs to be fleshed out more. At the same time that the reaction of the students in my philosophy class was a cause for concern, it is equally true that there was some satisfaction, even then, in knowing that they did feel free to speak their minds. After all, if students in an introductory philosophy class cannot voice their opinions and feelings about an issue, where else might they do so? What is of concern is not that they "indulged" in their right to express themselves, but what appeared to be the cause of their emotional reaction, namely the performative act of wearing the wedding ring. The reason this ought to be of concern and worked out still further is the following: Despite my sense of awareness of how I presented myself in the class, it was a "simple act" that provoked a totally unanticipated reaction. The act of wearing a wedding ring was, until then, not a performative issue for me, in part because of the privilege that made such acts for me simple in the first place.

Perhaps one could argue that in another class, with some other professor, these same students might not have so publicly voiced their reaction. I do feel some pride in this; however, the fact remains that a simple act was not, in fact, simple. So whatever pleasure I could derive from the students feeling "comfortable" enough to voice their reaction (confusion and disapproval) was muted by the response itself. In their assessment of me, of things academic and professorial, I failed to recognize fully the significance of my manner, my gestures and expressions. It was only upon hearing their response that I became aware of the complexity of my simple act.

Part of the reason I felt the sting of their reaction so strongly was because I had long been aware that how one acts is important. I had even consciously incorporated this perspective into my teaching. But until the act of wearing the wedding ring, I was ignorant of the significance of simple acts, acts performed within the complicated context of privilege that made such acts appear simple. So the sting was due, in part, to a sort of pride: I viewed myself as an ethical person who acted in the right way and yet found himself ignorant of the full complexity of "simple acts." As a thoughtful teacher, I was embarrassed by my own simple act of privilege and suddenly found it necessary to reconsider how I perfomed in and out of the classroom. But part of the reason for the intensity of the sting was due to the confusion concerning the choices I made in presenting myself, in the choices of strategies and techniques employed in the formation of myself, as it were.

In an interview just a year before his death in 1984, and later published under the title "On the Genealogy of Ethics: An Overview of Works in Progress," Michel Foucault told Paul Rabinow and Herbert Dryfus that the "subject" is constituted in, what he called, real practices, and that there is a technology of the formation of the self. Foucault comments that

> [t]echniques of the self, I believe can be found in all cultures in different forms. Just as it is necessary to study and compare the different techniques of the production of objects and the direction of men by men through government, one must also question techniques of the self. What makes the analysis of the techniques of the self

difficult is two things. First, the techniques of the self do not require the same material apparatus as the production of objects; therefore they are often invisible techniques. Second, they are frequently linked to the techniques for the direction of others. For example, if we take educational institutions, we realize that one is managing others and teaching them to manage themselves. (p. 370)

The need to be rigorous and thorough is clear. What I had to reevaluate were the various strategies and techniques I had used in the past, many of which were performed as simple acts of privilege. Although humbled and unsure exactly how to proceed, I nevertheless set out to analyze and hone what techniques and practices appeared to be of value for the classroom and beyond.

One important dimension to the proposed analysis was the need to seek out the many others who "have a story to tell," and to listen. The reevaluation of the techniques of the self that I deemed necessary would, in part, demand a genuine attention to the techniques employed by others attempting the same project, but others who, by dint of historical contingency, pursue their goal from the other side of privilege. In short, as Foucault insists, "one must also question techniques of the self." Thus to simply go about "reconsidering" one's own performative expressions (to merely ask "How am I doing?") without engaging with others and analyzing their techniques as well usually results in some kind of "reformed self," but one still operating within the isolating space of privilege. One of the givens of performing simple acts is the hazardous presumption of interconnection with those for whom the simple act is done. The act is seen as simple and innocuous by the perpetrator of the act precisely because of the belief in the *shared* context in which it is performed. This is why a nun's comment, "like a monkey," and a law professor's welcome, "Good morning, gentlemen," are viewed by too many people as little more than simple acts of endearment and acceptance. The supposed "common ground" on which we all stand often covers the "contested terrain," as Jackson and Jordan identify it, of the various regional modalities that do, in fact, constitute who and what we are. One needs to do more than simply reconsider a comment or a welcome; one needs to be willing to engage in rigorous, and sometimes painful, work. As Foucault warns us, self-analysis can be "an extremely painful exercise at first and requir[es] many cultural valorizations before ending up transformed into a positive activity" (p. 369).

Of course, engaging with others in the pursuit of questioning different techniques of the self should not be misconstrued as an invitation to perform yet another simple act of privilege—namely, engaging in a kind of consumer voyeurism. In her 1992 essay "Eating the Other: Desire and Resistance," bell hooks observes that

> [t]he commodification of Otherness has been so successful because it is offered as a new delight, more intense, more satisfying than normal ways of doing and feeling. Within commodity culture, ethnicity becomes spice, seasoning that can liven up the dull dish that is mainstream white culture. (p. 21)

To set out upon the ethical task of undoing the presumption of "simple acts" cannot be advanced by the unethical manipulation of merely "tasting" others in order to transgress or enhance, as bell hooks appraises it, the "dull dish that is mainstream white culture." The need to engage in observation, analysis, and consideration of different techniques of the self cannot fall prey to the anthropological imperialism of an earlier time. One would hope that the impact of feminism, critical race theory, and gender studies, among other strategies and criticisms, has cleared the way and that these perspectives provide some aid, if not a guarantee, to prevent missteps and abuses.

Regardless, however, of the risks and the possibility of mistakes, as Henry A. Giroux points out in his 1994 essay "Living Dangerously: Identity Politics and the New Cultural Racism":

> As we move into an age in which cultural space becomes unfixed, unsettled, porous, and hybrid, it becomes increasingly difficult either to defend notions of singular identity or to deny that different groups, communities, and people are increasingly bound to each other in a myriad of complex relationships. Modes of representation that legitimated a world of strict cultural separation, collective identities, and rigid boundaries seem hopelessly outdated as the urban landscape is being rewritten within new and shifting borders of identity, race, and ethnicity. (p. 40)

In other words, given the present-day reality of the various modes of contact and interaction negotiated by many different people living, working, teaching, and learning within and beyond the "urban landscape," what is required is a rigorous examination of the modes of representation employed by dominant (mainstream) culture and also, as I am arguing here, the modes of representation employed by those of us engaged in the critique of "dominant regimes."

Giroux has rightly identified the need for what he calls a critical pedagogy of representation and a representational pedagogy (Ibid., p. 41). As he explains it:

> In the first instance, I am referring to the various ways in which representations are constructed as a means of

comprehending the past through the present in order to legitimate and secure a particular view of the future. Pedagogically, this raises the question of how students can learn to interrogate the historical, semiotic, and relational dynamics involved in the production of various regimes of representations and their respective politics. In other words, a pedagogy of representation focuses on demystifying the act and process of representing by revealing how meanings are produced within relations of power that narrate identities through history, social forms and modes of ethical address that appear objective, universally valid, and consensual. (Ibid., p. 47)

For those committed to a "critical pedagogy" there is no clearer articulation of the project. But I am suggesting that there is also a need, for those of us involved with this educational strategy, to "interrogate" our own "simple acts" of representation, as well as others. The goal here is to incorporate Butler, Foucault, hooks, and Giroux in a way that allows for the possibility of performing acts that support a pedagogy of representation and a representational pedagogy.

What such acts might look like can differ depending upon the context and the regimes being challenged or called into question. But in every case where the simple act is somehow being "subverted" and its simplicity exposed, it is safe to say that the performative gesture or expression that brings this about must look different; namely, it must look challenging. Whatever strategies (acts) we choose to challenge the dominant (hegemonic) construction of identity, we must attempt, as Butler claims, to

locate strategies of subversive repetition enabled by those constructions, to affirm the local possibilities of intervention through participating in precisely those practices of repetition that constitute identity and, therefore, present the immanent possibility of contesting them. (Ibid., p. 147)

Thus the affirmative acts employed will, of necessity, be acts of repetition, acts that invert or disrupt in their very repetition of the "simple acts" that typically constitute identity. Therefore these "affirmative acts" are simultaneously voicing criticism and affirmation, a dynamic that demands thoughtfulness and practice.

Noting the difficulty of such acts and practices, Chandra Talpace Mohanty, in her 1994 essay "On Race and Voice," writes:

Clearly, this process is very complicated pedagogically, for such teaching must address questions of audience, voice, power and evaluation, while retaining a focus on the material being taught. Teaching practices must also combat the pressures of professionalization, normalization, and standardization, the very pressures of expectations that implicitly aim to manage and discipline pedagogies so that teacher behaviors are predictable (and perhaps controllable) across the board. (p. 153)

The task of such teaching is arguably daunting, if not outright intimidating. The need to think through the complicated issues of audience, voice, power, and the rest that Mohanty identifies requires rigorous and sophisticated analysis, commitment, and ability. Knowing the importance of these issues is a necessary but not sufficient condition for being able to successfully "subvert" the simple acts that occur in the classroom and to perform otherwise. There are certainly more than enough stories of teachers and professors entering the classroom ready to dismantle the hegemonic ideology and structure of patriarchal, capitalist, white supremist power, only to alienate their students through various simple acts of sexism, racism, class, and academic elitism. Here knowledge is as important as always, but the focus must be on the performative expressions that will or will not allow for Giroux's "critical pedagogy of representation" to unfold.

I have already suggested that one important way to address some of the issues just mentioned is by listening to others who "have a story to tell"—in this case, those who have something to say this side of privilege. This does not in any way mean only those who have been so marked or designated as "officially" this side of privilege have the right (the privilege?) to tell their story, thereby silencing others or rendering what those others have to say as less important or significant. Diana Fuss astutely observes in her essay "Essentialism in the Classroom" that

> [no]where are the related issues of essence, identity and experience so highly charged and so deeply politicized as they are in the classroom. Personal consciousness, individual oppression, lived experience—in short, identity politics—operate in the classroom both to authorize and to de-authorize speech. Experience emerges as the essential truth of the individual subject, and personal "identity" metamorphoses into knowledge. Who we are becomes what we know; ontology shades into epistemology. (p. 113)

What we ought to be striving toward is the "authorization" of those narratives that contest the hegemony of simple acts, and the participation of those whose expressions and gestures create a greater possibility for genuine teaching and learning. There is no point, in the attempt to overcome the presumption of the simple acts of privilege, to wrongly privilege only those stories and individuals who somehow automatically and reductively become the voices of opposition. The historical context and regional modalities of discursively constituted identities, as Butler puts it, are too complex and complicated for this to be the case.

Yet the fact remains that there is a real need (an ethical imperative) to disrupt and challenge the simple acts of privilege, and that one of the ways to begin this process is by listening to and acknowledging those for whom such acts are not simple. So clearly, for a white, heterosexual, male, tenured professor of relative financial security this means reading, listening to, and speaking with, among others, people of color. This, however, is not to suggest that only heterosexual white male academics should be challenging the presumption of their simple acts of privilege. People in different locations, occupying varying positions of power, also need to acknowledge the performance of their simple acts (their sexist, racist, homophobic, class elitist acts); *all teachers* need to confront power, the presumption of authority, the way they "act" in class. Each teacher ought to consider and reconsider the performative dynamics of their teaching in light of the critique of the simple acts of privilege suggested here.

Perhaps one of the most famous, and accessible, considerations of a simple act is Paulo Freire's criticism of the "banking concept" of education. His critique of the simple act of filling the minds of students with information "deposited" by a teacher is formulated in the second chapter of his now classic *Pedagogy of the Oppressed*. In this chapter he offers us a reconsideration of the dynamics of instruction, one predicated on dialogue rather than the sole narration of the teacher. As Cornel West notes in his 1993 commentary, titled "Paulo Freire":

> *Pedagogy of the Oppressed* was a world-historical event for counter-hegemonic theorists and activist in search of new ways to link social theory to narratives of human

freedom. This complex lineage led Freire to put a premium on dialogue, the construction of new subjects of history and the creation of new social possibilities in history.... Freire's project of democratic dialogue is attuned to the concrete operations of power (in and out of the classroom) and grounded in the painful yet empowering process of conscientization. This process embraces a critical demystifying moment in which structures of domination are laid bare and political engagement is imperative. (p. 179)

For some, Paulo Freire's challenge and disruption of the teacher's simple act of privilege, of being the sole narrator and subject in the classroom, are threats to the law and order of the education establishment and the very purpose of education, as Foucault notes, of teaching students how to *manage* themselves. For progressive educators, for transgressive educators, as bell hooks calls them, Freire's critique of the "banking system" of education offers us a powerful example of how to challenge the presumption of, in this case, the simple act of imparting information, of speaking monologically and rendering students silent.

Another way of engaging in the process of reconsideration of one's presumption of the simple acts of privilege is suggested by Freire's fellow Brazilian Augusto Boal, a theater director, writer, theorist, and educator. In his powerful collection of exercises *Games for Actors and Non-Actors*, Boal offers us some strategies and opportunities to explore and reconsider ourselves *in action*. The "games" contained in his book offer us the chance to act—that is, to perform and to take action, as opposed to merely reacting in a habitual manner. In so doing, in so experiencing ourselves in the act of the game, we give ourselves, our bodies, the occasion and space, as Boal claims, to begin a process of "de-mechanization."

According to Boal,

> Like all human beings, the actor acts and reacts accord-
> ing to mechanisms. For this reason, we must start with
> the "de-mechanisation," the re-tuning (or de-tuning) of
> the actor [teacher]. . . . (Ibid., p. 41)

The reason for "reacting to mechanisms" has to do primarily
with repetition. As he points out,

> [t]heater can also be the repetitve acts of daily life. We
> perform the play of breakfast, the scene of going to work,
> the act of working, the epilogue of supper, the epic of
> Sunday lunch with the family, etc.; like actors in a long
> run of a successful show, repeating the same lines to the
> same partners, executing the same movements, at the
> same times, thousands of times over. Life can become a
> series of mechanisations, as rigid and as lifeless as the
> movements of a machine. (Ibid., p. xxv)

Thus one of the purposes of the "games" is to provoke what
the French philosopher Gilles Deleuze refers to as a repetition
with a difference, the disruption of the mechanization of
everyday (habitual) acts. With the games, Boal offers us
(nonactors) techniques to achieve a similar goal sought by
Butler, hooks, and Giroux, namely to confront, disrupt, and
destabilize the dominant regimes of representation and to
affirm possibilities for other constructions and representations
in the process of performing "subversive acts." Though each
of these thinkers, critics, and writers has a different emphasis,
each understands and utilizes the performative dimension of
representation as part of her or his critique and strategy
toward a positive political agenda.

  While Boal offers a no less theoretically sophisticated

critique or strategy than of those just mentioned, his "theatrical" approach allows us to physically and emotionally experiment with the techniques of the self that occur when using a performative—in his words, a theatrical—language. This is so, according to Boal, because

> [t]he theatrical language is the most essential human language. Everything that actors do, we do throughout our lives, always and everywhere. Actors talk, move, dress to suit the setting, express ideas, reveal passions—just as we all do in our daily lives. The only difference is that actors are conscious that they are using the language of theater, and are thus better able to turn it to their advantage, whereas the woman or man in the street do [not] know that they are speaking theater, just as Molière's Monsieur Jourdain (La Bourgeois Gentilhomme) was unaware that he spoke prose. (Ibid., p. xxx)

The goal here is to have teachers become more aware through a variety of techniques, including the "theatrical" exercises and games suggested by Boal. Through such challenges of what I have been calling the presumption of the simple acts of privilege, teachers can begin to use the full array of possibilities available to them to further positive communicative engagement and to overcome, or at least confront, the pathology of communicative acts performed naively and habitually.

It is sadly disturbing that consideration of the performative aspect of teaching meets with such resistance and hostility. While it is understandable when such a reaction comes from those on the right, it is even more disheartening when liberal and even progressive pedagogues resist. Of course, to play such "games" would mean the beginning of demechanization and subversive acts of repetition, and with this would come challenges from others as well as self-criticism. But one needs to confront the presumption of those simple acts of privilege that have sustained one's position, even if it is a "liberal" or a "progressive" position. To begin a pedagogy that, to use Giroux's term, is "critical" and promoting democratic values, one needs to be willing to confront the simple acts that have allowed for an identity and teaching style that are situated in the complicated context that is the United States today.

When I walked into my philosophy class wearing my wedding ring, I was engaged in the serious and respectable task of working with students to assist them in thinking critically about the content that they were going to read that semester. I did not, however, fully consider the possibility that *I* also was part of what they would be reading, and that I had the additional task of assisting them read me. How I spoke, how I dressed—in short, how I acted—informed and influenced the content of the course in important and necessary ways. It was as much my obligation to be rigorous and thorough about how I presented myself as it was to be so regarding the material for the course. The need for teachers, at every level of instruction, to be mindful of how they perform can no longer be ignored or relegated to the realm of "mere process." At a time when the presumption of the simple acts of privilege still dominates the teaching profession (as well as our culture as a whole), the demand that teachers must begin to consider their actions in and out of the classroom is as much an ethical demand as it is a political or a pedagogical demand, and we ought not be daunted by the intersection of these three domains of action. For too long, the right has laid claim to this very intersection and as a result has wrongly influenced the direction of education in the United States. It is time for progressive educators to acknowledge the validity of this intersection and begin to simply act accordingly.

6.

Why Multiculturalism (*Still*)?

"Multiculturalism" is a term that provokes strong responses, both positive and negative. To some it represents a flash point for controversy, while to others it offers a ray of hope toward addressing the many complex issues teachers face every day. Over the years, journalists, political commentators, and even philosophers have weighed in with their differing opinions of endorsement and rejection. The reasons for the emotional attacks on and passionate advocacy for multiculturalism are as diverse as those vilifying it or supporting its implementation. Yet despite all the attention, "multiculturalism" remains a volatile term typically misused and often incorrectly defined by those on both sides of the debate. After eight years of directing the Graduate Program in Urban and Multicultural Education the College of Mount Saint Vincent in the Bronx, I have heard, and made it my business to read, just about every conceivable argument for and against multiculturalism. In what follows, I would like to offer my response to the often asked question Why multiculturalism (*still*)?

In his straightforward yet vexing book, *We Are All Multiculturalists Now*, renowned Harvard professor emeritus of sociology and education Nathan Glazer matter-of-factly announces

that multiculturalism in education—so strongly denounced by so many powerful voices in American life, by
historians, publicists, labor leaders, intellectuals, the
occasion for so many major battles in American education during the nineties, and so much at odds with the
course of American culture, society and education at least
up until the 1960s—has, in a word won. I do not assert
this either to sound an alarm over this victory or to cele-
brate it. (p. 4)

According to Glazer, he is simply stating the "fact" that the
"culture wars" have been won by the proponents of multiculturalism, and the thrust of his book is that everyone (read
"the losers") will have to ride it out. As he puts it,

[m]any terms have thus arisen to encompass the reality
that groups of different origin all form part of the
American population, and in varying degrees part of a
common culture and society. Multiculturalism is just the
latest in this sequence of terms describing how American
society, particularly American education, should respond
to its diversity. (Ibid., p. 8)

In short, Glazer's view of multiculturalism could be stated this
way: It is "just" the latest fad to sweep through the ever-
oscillating political field of education. Glazer's implicit
advice—as many seasoned teachers have learned over the
course of enduring tumultuous battles involving changes in
curriculum, standards, and policy—is to seek solace from
these sagacious words, "this, too, shall pass."

Glazer's assessment of multiculturalism is by no means the
typical knee-jerk neoconservative dismissal that usually finds
its way onto the editorial pages of liberal and conservative
newspapers and journals alike. But he does, however, end up

voicing the now very familiar, basic criticism that multi-culturalism is merely the most recent, and flawed, attempt to deal with the diversity of the United States. Multiculturalism, from this perspective, is primarily understood as little more than the newfangled effort by those who have felt wronged or otherwise excluded from "mainstream" representation to gain political ground. As Glazer concludes,

> [m]ulticulturalism is *the price* America is paying for its inability or unwillingness to incorporate into its society African Americans, in the same way and to the same degree it has incorporated so many groups. (Ibid., p. 147; emphasis added)

Multiculturalism, therefore, is considered "the price America is paying" for failing, whether intentionally or not, to incorporate African Americans into mainstream society. Glazer's view, which is critical of racism, reveals his liberal roots, yet it also reveals his neoconservative inclination to attach negative significance to strategies and efforts that confront the racists status quo. Why, for example, consider multiculturalism "the price"? Why attach this negative connotation to what many consider a positive reform movement in education?

For Glazer and others, the problem with multiculturalism is that it is divisive; it creates a "balkanized" conception and experience of ethnic "cultures" that undermine the goal of a common and shared culture of American society.

> The problems of divisiveness that multiculturalism raises at the level of the curriculum, or the school, or the culture, cannot be settled within the curriculum, the school, or the larger culture. The "culture wars" reflect many things, but when it comes to the division of blacks and others, they reflect a hard reality that none of us

wants, that all of us want to see disappear, but that none of us knows how to overcome. It is only change in that larger reality that will reduce multiculturalism to a passing phase in the complex history of the making of an American nation from many strands. (Ibid., p. 161)

In expressing this position, Glazer, in the final sentences of his book, certainly suggests, if not directly states, that multiculturalism is a problem "whites" will have to endure until such time as the real problem "all of us want to see disappear" in fact disappears.

Oddly enough, Glaser's point amounts to the following proposition: Multiculturalism will remain a divisive force in our society—for the foreseeable future, anyway—as long as whites and blacks remain divided. Glazer seems quite content, however, with blaming multiculturalism for being divisive in a culture that is already divided. What he never seems to consider are those aspects of multiculturalism that would foster "solidarity" in the face of the historical divisiveness endured by so many for so long.

Glazer is not the only distinguished scholar to come down on the side critical of multiculturalism. Pulitzer Prize-winning historian Arthur Schlesinger Jr. also sees multiculturalism as a threat to the American experiment. In his best-selling and critically acclaimed book *The Disuniting of America: Reflections on a Multicultural Society*, Schlesinger warns that

> [t]he ethnic upsurge (it can hardly be called a revival because it was unprecedented) began as a gesture of protest against the Anglocentric culture. It became a cult, and today it threatens to become a counterrevolution against the original theory of America as "one people," a common culture, a single nation. (p. 43)

Like Glazer, Schlesinger merges "the ethnic upsurge" with multiculturalism and sees both as "threats" to America; no wonder so many consider multiculturalism unpatriotic. It is one thing to suggest that a particular strategy for claiming one's (or one's "group's") value may have some "negative" implications or consequences. It is quite another, however, to emphatically state that such a strategy is a cult movement that threatens to evolve into a counterrevolution against the hope of achieving an America that is united—with a common culture—a counterrevolution against the United States becoming, as he puts it, a "single nation."

Unlike the numerous demagogues of the right who seek to restore America, seeing only ungrateful minorities taking advantage of "white guilt," Schlesinger (as does Glazer) represents a different kind of criticism, but one that ultimately plays into the hands of those political conservatives who see nothing but a ruinous future for America if multiculturalism prevails. For all these critics, multiculturalism somehow undoes or redoes history in an attempt to advance the status of particular ethnic groups over and above Anglo-American contributions to the foundation of America. Used (or abused) in this way, history is turned into a weapon aimed at destroying the unity of the United States. "History as weapon," Schlesinger tells us,

> is an abuse of history. The high purpose of history is not the presentation of self nor the vindication of identity but the recognition of complexity and the search for knowledge. (Ibid., p. 72)

Appealing to the "high purpose" of history, Schlesinger rejects challenges ("abuses") that call into question the significance ("overcelebration," as Donaldo Macedo calls it) of Anglo-American contributions. Schlesinger equates some questionable assertions by Afrocentrists as outright violations of the moral purpose of history, while much more generously forgiving the myths, inaccuracies, and lies that have been presented in the name of the "recognition of complexity and the search for knowledge."

Schlesinger also suggests that Afrocentrists and multiculturalists approach history "as therapy" to elevate the spirit of students of color, and he goes on to argue that "[t]he use of history as therapy means the corruption of history as history" (Ibid., p. 93). Interestingly in his rejection, he never gives any real credence to the possibility that learning the complexity of history and searching for knowledge are themselves uplifting when not corrupted by prejudice and disrespect. Schlesinger is unimpressed with the efforts of Afrocentrists and multiculturalists struggling to find pedagogical strategies to promote such learning; he is suspicious of the real value of such methods and efforts. "After all," Schlesinger wonders,

> what good will it do young black Americans to take African names, wear African costumes, and replicate African rituals, to learn by music and mantras, rhythm and rapping, to reject standard English, to hear that because their minds work differently a first-class education is not for them? Will such training help them to understand democracy better? (Ibid., p. 93)

What Schlesinger presents is a picture of alternative historical narratives as necessarily leading to such "useless" and "counterproductive" activities as wearing African "costumes," replicating African "rituals," rejecting standard English, and doubting the viability of a first-class education. Nowhere does he consider that a rigorous historical analysis that challenges some of the "myths" of American history might lead to greater understanding of the progress of our democracy, and provide a vehicle for many new learners to make "historical sense" of America. Besides, one might legitimately ask, what "good" does it "do" for young white Americans to be given "Anglo" names, wear European "costumes," and replicate Judeo-Christian "rituals"? Of course, the "good" such practices "do" involves meaningfully integrating oneself and one's "group" into the everyday lived experience of citizenship and nationhood. The fact that the visibility of the different Afro-American "styles," "rituals," and "interests" strikes Schlesinger as intuitively counterproductive to better understanding our democracy only emphasizes the presumption of the higher value, significance, and neutrality of the Anglo-European influences on our national identity. This is not to say that Anglo-European influences are unimportant and not essential to the genesis and development of the United States. It also does not suggest that all things Anglo are *prima facie* racist, sexist, or harmful to peoples of other than European descent. Rather, the point is simply to insist on the recognition that "other," non-Anglo, influences are of historical and ethical value, too, and that other groups have made genuine and lasting contributions to our democracy. The fear that appreciating, or even acknowledging, non-Anglo American influences and values automatically diminishes European glory and threatens our democracy seems at best overreactive and at worst suspiciously racist.

Unfortunately, rather than seriously considering the benefits of multiculturalism, the prevailing attitude of those critical of such a strategy is that it is a perspective that has been taken to an extreme and is now out of control. "Almost any idea, carried to its extreme," says former assistant U.S. secretary of education Diane Ravitch in her essay "Multiculturalism: E Pluribus Plures,"

> can be made pernicious, and this is what is happening now to multiculturalism. Today, pluralistic multicultural-

ism must contend with a new, particularistic multiculturalism. The pluralists seek a richer common culture;
the particularists insist that no common culture is possible or desirable. . . . Advocates of particularism propose
an ethnocentric curriculum to raise the self-esteem and
academic achievement of children from racial and ethnic
minority backgrounds. Without any evidence, they claim
that children from minority backgrounds will do well in
school only if they are immersed in a positive, prideful
version of their ancestral culture. (p. 276)

In her criticism, Ravitch is in keeping with Glazer and
Schlesinger, but suggests that she is a supporter of something
called "pluralistic multiculturalism"—that is, multiculturalism
prior to being "carried to its extreme." To hide her overall
rejection of multiculturalism, Ravitch sets up this falsely
bifurcated multiculturalism with the "reasonable" portion
losing out to the extreme version. Thus we are forced to
reject multiculturalsim "today" because the radical other
version has gotten out of hand and threatens students with
methods and content that are advocated "without any
evidence" of their value.

Ravitch hits hard, claiming that

the particularistic version of multiculturalism is
unabashedly filiopietistic and deterministic. It teaches
children that their identity is determined by their
"cultural genes." That something in their blood or their
race memory or their cultural DNA defines who they are
and what they may achieve. That the culture in which
they live is not their own culture, even though they were
born here. That American culture is "Eurocentric," and
therefore hostile to anyone whose ancestors are not
European. (Ibid., p. 277)

She, like Glazer and Schlesinger, merges (and confuses) multi-culturalism with a particular position advocated by *some* Afrocentrics and argues the need to reject *both* for the harm they cause our nation. By refusing to distinguish between multiculturalism and other strategies attempting to confront the prejudice and disrespect to be found in and out of the classrooms in schools across America, Ravitch plays into the fears and anger of those struggling to restore, if in a somewhat reformed manner, the nobility of the damaged image of America after the challenge to Eurocentrism.

In his direct response to Ravitch, noted professor of African-American studies at Temple University Molefi Kete Asante argues, in his essay "Multiculturalism: An Exchange," that Ravitch wrongly

> posits a pluralist multiculturalism—a redundancy—then suggests a particularistic multiculturalism—an oxy-moron—in order to beat a dead horse. The ideas are non-starters because they have no reality in fact. I wrote the first book in this country on transracial communication and edited the first handbook on intercultural communica-tion, and I am aware of the categories Professor Ravitch seeks to forge. She claims that the pluralist multicultural-ism believes in pluralism and the particularist multi-culturalism in particularism. Well multiculturalism in education is almost self-defining. It is simply the idea that the educational experience should reflect the diverse cul-tural heritage of our system of knowledge. I have con-tended that such is not the case and cannot be the case until teachers know more about the African-American, Native American, Latino, and Asian experiences. (pp. 304–5)

Asante provides a clear and simple response to Ravitch's false splitting of multiculturalism. An Afrocentric who is also an advocate of multiculturalism, Asante gives voice to the issue facing American educators, namely the need to know more history and do more than pay lip service to the cultural history of our system of knowledge and values. Of course, how this might be achieved and why it is of value are the very goals of multiculturalism.

One interesting and frustrating aspect of the many attacks by those criticizing multiculturalism is their refusal to ever meaningfully engage the practitioners and theorists of this educational movement. For example, of the three critics mentioned here, the only one Nathan Glazer ever mentions is Professor James A. Banks, and he does so only in passing, and none mentions the important work of Professor Sonia Nieto, author of *Affirming Diversity: The Sociopolitical Context of Multicultural Education*. This is hard to believe given the significant place Banks and Nieto occupy in the field, and the clarity and usefulness of their work. Professor Banks, in particular, has been quite influential in both defining and promoting what multicultural education is and can do for all American students and teachers. One would assume that his work specifically warrants comment, even if critical, from these detractors, but none seems willing to pursue the issues raised by Banks. Perhaps the reason why critics of multiculturalism refuse to discuss his and others' work involved with multicultural education has to do with lack of knowledge about the field itself, but, as I suspect, it also may be due to attempts to distort what multiculturalism is in order to reject its challenges and proposals.

Banks's assessment of the situation is expressed in his book *An Introduction to Multicultural Education*. According to Banks,

[t]he bitter canon debate in the popular press and in several widely reviewed books has overshadowed the progress in multicultural education that has been made

during the last two decades. The debate has also perpetuated the harmful misconceptions about theory and practice in multicultural education. It has consequently increased racial and ethnic tension and trivialized the field's remarkable accomplishments in theory, research, and curriculum development. The truth about the development and attainments of multicultural education needs to be told, for the sake of balance, scholarly integrity, and accuracy. (p. 5)

Sadly, the work of Glazer, Schlesinger, and Ravitch, never mind the incendiary work of Dinesh D'Sousa, William Bennett, and others, ignores, misunderstands, and distorts much, if not all, of what multiculturalism has to offer. In addition, the media have seized upon the crossfire and typically have nonmulticulturalists, among them controversial Professor Leonard Jefferies of City College of New York, as the only respondents. This might make for "good" television debate but hardly allows for the goals and principles of multiculturalism to get a fair hearing by a curious public.

Banks addresses many of the misconceptions promulgated by various critics. He notes, for example, that multiculturalism

is not an ethnic- or gender-specific movement, but is a movement designed to empower all students to become knowledgeable, caring, and active citizens in a deeply troubled and ethnically polarized nation and world. (Ibid.)

As such, multiculturalism is meant for every student and teacher confronted by a curriculum and teaching method that refuse to acknowledge the complexity and diversity of the world in which we all live, learn, and teach. Banks further notes that the claim that multiculturalism is somehow against

Western culture and civilization is absurd. The simple fact is that most of the writers who are important to a "multicultural" approach are themselves "Western." It is often overlooked, if not purposely ignored, but

> [m]ulticultural education itself is a thoroughly Western movement. It grew out of a civil rights movement grounded in Western democratic ideals such as freedom, justice, and equality. Multicultural education seeks to expand for all people ideals that were meant for an elite few at the nation's beginning. (Ibid., p. 6)

What critics such as Glazer, Schlesinger, and Ravitch have in common is the belief that because multiculturalism challenges the historical distortions of an exclusively Anglocentric perspective and argues for a more accurate inclusion of non-Anglo-American people and influences, multiculturalism is against Western culture, against the United States, and therefore unpatriotic. Part of the problem is that these and other critics are unable to even conceive of a "Western" connection to multiculturalism. They simply assume that any "demand" for changes in the curriculum that includes a genuine integration of Anglo and non-Anglo influences necessarily demeans and threatens Western civilization and the moral stability of the United States. To the contrary, as Banks suggests, multiculturalism is a movement to expand the full scope of "Western" culture and allow for the possibility of a less distorted "global" perspective.

Banks articulates five areas or "dimensions" of multicultural education: (1) content integration; (2) the knowledge construction process; (3) prejudice reduction; (4) equity pedagogy; and (5) empowering school culture and school structure. These five discrete but connected and integrated domains spell out the purpose and scope of multicultural education.

The first dimension, content integration,

> deals with the extent to which teachers use examples and
> content from a variety of cultures and groups to illustrate
> key concepts, principles, generalizations and theories in
> their subject area or discipline. (Ibid., p. 14)

By using examples, data, and information from different cultures and groups (both from within and beyond the United States), teachers can introduce concepts, theories, principles, and values in their subject area and discipline in a way that promotes richer connections and positive intercultural and historical perspectives. Banks does note, however, that many people (perhaps too many) directly involved with teaching or writing about and debating the merits of multiculturalism often wrongly limit multiculturalism to just this one dimension.

The problem with so limiting multiculturalism in this way is twofold. On the one hand, limiting multicultural education to this one dimension ignores the other aspects of this teaching strategy that are equally important and therefore restricts its scope and range. On the other hand, limiting multiculturalism to this one dimension, according to Banks, also bolsters the erroneous impression that multiculturalism is relevant exclusively to teachers of social studies or the language arts, and not to those teaching science. Banks argues that this bias, in turn, gives critics of multiculturalism the opening to argue that when it comes to "objective" facts and information (e.g., $2 + 2 = 4$ and other "hard" facts), the role and significance of "cultural" information is of little or no value at all. Unfortunately, such a line of arguing ultimately leads to rejecting multiculturalism because of its alleged lack of applicability to the "real things that matter." It also often leads to rejection because of the supposedly subjective (and arbitrary) nature of infusing the curriculum with examples and content from "other cultures into a given subject area or discipline."

I think Banks is absolutely right in noting the perception and consequent attitude of some schoolteachers, and of most critics who claim that because content integration is of significance "only" to social studies and language arts teachers, it therefore belies the educational value of multiculturalism by revealing its true subjective and arbitrary nature. Banks argues that it is only because these schoolteachers and critics refuse to recognize the other dimensions of multiculturalism that they are able to reject its application to the sciences. I think Banks's response is appropriate enough, but I believe he too readily surrenders the significance of content integration for the sciences.

Granted, Banks is justified in feeling confident that multiculturalism will prove its value to those teaching science when the other dimensions are appropriately considered and included as part of this educational strategy. As a result, he apparently feels comfortable giving up any claim of value here for the sciences. Yet the significance of using examples and content from other cultures and groups to illustrate principles, concepts, and theories of science should not be underestimated or abandoned so quickly.

Given that this chapter is not intended to be a disputation on content integration and the sciences, I will not attempt here a fully developed argument addressing the issue. I will, however, suggest why I believe that content integration is of a genuine usefulness (significance) for science teachers and, in doing so, also offer some rebuttal to critics attempting to reject multiculturalism by limiting it to content integration. Without attempting to lay out a multicultural science curriculum or enter into a lengthy debate over different notions of science and its methodolgy, I simply want to argue that content integration can be useful (i.e., intellectually and pedagogically significant) for science instruction.

As Banks points out, many critics of multicultural education, and even some teachers sympathetic to multiculturalism,
have argued that the introduction of examples and content
from other cultures and groups, as prescribed by content integration, artificially and ultimately unsuccessfully attempts to
demonstrate connections to the teaching of science. But even
a cursory review of the history of science suggests that
"cultural" temperament and attitude play some role in scientific research and exploration. Even the very notion of
"Western science" implies a meaningful distinction between it
and "non-Western science." But even within "Western
science" there is much that content integration could do to
prove useful in helping to explicate and discuss key concepts,
principles, and theories. For example, math teachers could
discuss the significance of the "discovery" of irrational
numbers for the ancient Greeks. What were the implications
of the existence of such a number for a culture such as the
Greeks? What were the possible consequences for the social
order and conventional morality? What was it about numbers
themselves that provoked the different Greek mathematicians
to pursue the "character" of even and odd numbers? What was
it about the Greeks that led them to follow such paths of
considerations?

A math teacher could easily and quite meaningfully introduce examples and content that are not widely known to most
American students (mainstream and nonmainstream alike) that
could assist them in their appreciation and understanding of
what is at stake when dealing with mathematics by looking at
an ancient culture. To let contemporary students know that the
entire existence of a rationally ordered universe (cosmos) was
jeopardized by the introduction of an entity identified as an
irrational number brings a meaning and an awareness to the
discussion of numbers in a way that is quite different if ignored.
Something real was at stake for the Greeks, and this was very
much an epochal, and therefore cultural, transformative

moment for them and that had lasting importance for all who followed. That some may argue that the Greeks are "our" cultural ancestors misses the point. First, the historical tradition identified as "Western" clearly includes many other cultures besides the Greeks; and second, the cultural-historical context in which the "Greeks" worked through "their" scientific issues (cosmological, biological, etc.) are certainly different—radically different, one might say—from today and the students studying today.

Similarly, introducing relevant information and content from Egyptian and Chinese "cultures" could prove of value. Discussing and examining agricultural, astronomical, and biological traditions would help students gain understanding of and insights into the world from multiple perspectives, one of the key goals of content integration. (Perhaps the inclusion of "other" such content would better prepare future doctors to confront the "Western vs. Eastern" medicine debate.) In addition, studying the techniques of Polynesian navigation could prove useful for discussing the plotting of "Cartesian" coordinates in relation to non-Euclidian geometry—that is, the "real" world.

None of this, however, is meant to artificially or gratuitously give "value" to content and examples from other cultures. Rather, the historical and scientific context they offer students could allow for greater involvement with, interest in, and understanding of scientific methodology and applications. Incorporating complex and diverse theories, principles, and concepts from other cultures would expose students to and allow them to consider a broader body of knowledge and better prepare them for further intellectual inquiry. Much more work in content integration is needed generally, but especially in the teaching of science.

The second dimension of multicultural education discussed by Banks directly flows from content integration and is identified as the knowledge construction process. This process

> relates to the extent to which teachers help students to
> understand, investigate, and determine how the implicit
> cultural assumptions, frames of references, perspectives,
> and biases within a discipline influence the ways in which
> knowledge is constructed within it. (Ibid.)

Unlike content integration, the knowledge construction
process is more complicated to explain, and demands an additional level of intellectual sophistication to understand.
Consequently, this dimension places an additional responsibility on teachers who are committed to teaching from a
multicultural perspective. In some sense, this dimension of
multicultural education represents a metapedagogical and
metamethodological issue for teachers. Because the knowledge construction process examines the various procedures
and assumptions, implicit cultural frames of references and
prejudices, this dimension is most closely associated with
current work being done in philosophy today influenced by
the late French philosopher Michel Foucault, and with those
who have been influenced by him in other disciplines, such as
anthropology and sociology. Oddly enough, Banks never
mentions Foucault by name in his book, though he does refer
to Sandra Harding and others who directly make use of
Foucault's work to do their own. This is a relatively minor
issue, but what is of more importance here and worth noting is
the fact that the examination of the knowledge construction
process has a long philosophical history and is not solely a
"postmodern" concern, as many critics of multiculturalism
would claim or imply.

Different philosophical traditions have explored the epistemological structures, assumptions, and prejudices of
numerous disciplines throughout the ages. This focus is what
has led to "paradigm" shifts and challenges to established
methods and concepts. From Plato through Nietszche, and
from Freud to Foucault, the "Western" tradition itself is a

history of the knowledge construction process. I mention this because many critics of multicultural education have suggested that the reevaluation and reconsideration of the nature and scope of knowledge have led to little else than the sort of nonsense made infamous by the Alan D. Sokal hoax.

Sokal, a repected left-progressive professor of physics at New York University, published an academic article titled "Transgressing the Boundaries: Toward a Transformative Hermeneutics of Quantum Gravity" in the well-known journal *Social Text*, involving a "postmodern critique" of science. Sokal feigned an attack against the objectivity of science, making controversial claims masked by the jargon of postmodernism. Then, in *Lingua Franca*, a journal that follows the foibles of and antics occurring in academia, Sokal exposed himself as having published an unrigorous bit of trash and goes on to criticize the absurdity of "postmodernity," along with those using it to advance various critiques of the knowledge construction process. Whatever his true motivation, Sokal gave many adversaries of multiculturalism and postmodernism ammunition to attack from various fronts. Yet despite the blacklash Sokal inflicted on those offering genuine and rigorous inquiry into the epistemological (and ontological) assumptions, structures, and prejudices at play in scientific research and in other disciplines, such work continues. In fact, one could argue that the "Western" tradition, to its credit, is a tradition marked by such debate and controversy over the status and order of things, and so educators must not shy away from the intellectual richness and significance of this tradition and continue to examine the knowledge construction process.

The third dimension identified by Banks is prejudice reduction. For him

> [t]his dimension focuses on the characteristics of students' racial attitudes and how they can be modified by teaching methods and materials. (Ibid.)

The goal and the significance of this dimension are straightforward enough. Children become aware of racial identities at an early age; it is the aim of prejudice reduction to help students successfully achieve appropriate attitudes concerning race and ethnicity. Like content integration, prejudice reduction is easily explained and identified: to reduce prejudice. But here, too, I believe, Banks attempts to avoid antagonism toward multicultural education by not extending the scope of prejudice reduction to include more rather than less, namely explicitly tackling homophobia.

Just as Banks understandably attempted to avert criticism of content integration by ceding the limit of its significance to social studies and the language arts, here he similarly tries to avoid problems by not including prejudice against sexual orientation as explicitly part of prejudice reduction. Though understandable, the lacuna left by this avoidance must be addressed—ignoring it would undermine the true scope and nature of multiculturalism.

The fourth area discussed by Banks is equity pedagogy. Such a pedagogy

> exists when teachers modify their teaching in ways that will facilitate the academic achievement of students from diverse racial, cultural, and social-class groups. This includes using a variety of teaching styles that are consistent with the wide range of learning styles within various cultural and ethnic groups. (Ibid.)

This dimension of multicultural education identified by Banks is the very one that Schlesinger and Ravitch allude to in their criticism of multiculturalism. For them and those who agree with them, this aspect of multiculturalism leads to the "dumbing" down of the curriculum and the inclusion of pedagogical styles and practices that are greeted with suspicion, if not outright contempt.

Though less straightforward than content integration and prejudice reduction, the goal of equity pedagogy is clear: to better facilitate learning by acknowledging and addressing the differences among diverse racial, cultural, and social-class groups.

The fifth and final dimension Banks calls to our attention is empowering school culture and social structure. This dimension

> describes the process of restructuring the culture and organization of the school so that students from diverse racial, ethnic, and social groups will experience educational equality and empowerment. This dimension of multicultural education involves conceptualizing the school as a unit of change and making structural changes within the school environment so that students from all social-class, racial, ethnic, and gender groups will have an equal opportunity for success. (Ibid., p. 17)

This dimension of multicultural education makes it obvious that unless the entire school is organized and structured as a positive learning environment for all students, academic success will be at risk. The whole school community must be committed to and knowledgeable of the other dimensions of multicultrual education and be willing and able to implement them if academic success for all students is to be achieved.

Multicultural education as Banks lays it out is multidimensional and predicated on the foundations of democratic principles and social justice that are at the core of our nation's soul, but have not always been equally available to all citizens because of the historical gap between such ideals and actual institutional practices, and structures. Multicultural education then is, as Banks defines it,

[a]n educational reform movement whose major goal is to restructure curricula and educational institutions so that students from diverse social-class, racial, and ethnic groups—as well as both gender groups—will experience equal educational opportunities. (Ibid., p. 116)

But as we have seen, this effort has been met with opposition from a number of fronts. As a result, multiculturalists are forced to answer the accusations of conservative critics who are misinformed, antagonistic, and driven by a vision of nationalism that consumes all differences in the name of "shared values" and "common culture." What makes things worse is that there are those on the left who also confuse things with their "support" of and attacks on multiculturalism.

An example of the sort of friendly confusion alluded to above can be witnessed by examining the numerous volumes by academics often identified, in some way or another, as postmodernists, and usually professors of philosophy or English. Efforts to work out many of the subtle, and not so subtle, issues associated with feminism, queer theory, and identity politics among other domains of inquiry that explore, confront, and offer alternatives to traditional "representations" and "constructions" of different subjects have been wrongly categorized under the rubric "multiculturalism." This is unfortunate for a variety of reasons, but particularly because these efforts and modes of inquiry further damage the possibility for genuine reform of the curriculum and educational institutions that are the focus of multicultural education. This is not to say that these modes of inquiry are not important to multiculturalism but are too often mistaken for it.

For instance, Cynthia Willett has edited an interesting book of essays titled *Theorizing Multiculturalism: A Guide to the Current Debate*, but it is not a collection that addresses multiculturalism, theoretically or otherwise. Instead, this volume places important philosophical discussions about "post-Hegelian dialectics," "post-Marxism," "Continental and analytical feminism," "corporeal logic sexuate being," and "postcolonialism and ethnicity," among other topics, within the multicultural debate. So when someone interested in finding out about multiculturalism reads this book, she or he will in fact be led into the valuable, complex, and unfortunately confusing domain of philosophical debate that ultimately offers little by way of "theorizing multiculturalism" as such. How could it? The people writing about it are unfamilar with or unwilling to acknowledge the history of multiculturalism and its primary theorists. The discussions and analyses are interesting and under the right conditions could prove useful; but left standing alone they only add to the general confusion over multiculturalism and give its enemies more ammunition to fight with, namely the claim that multiculturalism is just the pedagogical front of postmoderism.

To repeat, the essays in *Theorizing Multiculturalism* are written by some of the most respected names in philosophy today, and it is a volume that is of value even to multiculturalists with a background in the philosophical traditions employed and discussed. It does not, however, advance the theoretical discussion of multiculturalism within its social, political, and theoretical context. Instead, it hints at ways in which philosophical analysis might be changed or expanded when discussing topics and issues that emerge from multiculturalism. The very title of Willett's book offers a clue that here, too, multiculturalism is in need of "being theorized" and in the process is wrongly identified and usurped rather than acknowledged as a useful (theoretical) mode of analysis in its own right; thus the "friendly confusion."

Another example of this sort of book is a volume edited by Amy Gutmann titled *Multiculturalism: Examining the Politics of*

Recognition. In this volume Gutmann offers readers an essay by the eminent Canadian philosopher Charles Taylor and commentary by professors of religion and philosophy. In addition, a second section that includes essays by K. Anthony Appiah and Jürgen Habermas. Once again, we are offered important and interesting discussions and analyses by notable scholars. But, like Willett's collection, this volume is a philosopher's "take" on multiculturalism and is contextualized within the debate over the politics of recognition. It is not a philosophical analysis directly influenced by multiculturalism, but instead is, in my opinion, a discussion about the politics of multiculturalism, a valuable debate but nevertheless also adding to the friendly (and not so friendly) confusion. Gutmann's volume offers much that could prove useful to those interested in such a philosophical discussion and to those involved with multiculturalism interested in learning what philosophers are saying about it, but it is not a multicultural philosophical analysis, and therefore adds to the confusion because it, too, makes the connection between multiculturalism and postmodernism without ever defining multiculturalism as it exists in the United States.

Thus Gutmann's and Willett's volumes are vexing to those of us involved with multiculturalism because of the obvious and simple reason that, though friendly, they add to the confusion and distrust associated with the issue. Just as the conservative critics make accusations and belittle the significance of multiculturalism, so too do "friendly" volumes by philosophers and others directly and indirectly undermine the importance of multiculturalism by ignoring it while talking in its name. As acknowledged, these books are of value and do discuss important issues related to the philosophical and theoretical issues of multiculturalism but are not themselves necessarily engaged with multiculturalism. Thus they also, unintentionally, devalue the importance and significance of this educational reform movement by "providing" the theoretical sophistication one can only assume multiculturalism must lack on it own. By offering the weight of philosophical analysis, which itself does not clearly utilize a multicultural perspective, the theoretical and political forces of multiculturalism are at least weakened, if not dismissed. Perhaps if someone would first write about philosophy in the age of multiculturalism—that is, discussing how and in what ways philosophical analysis is different because of multiculturalism (if so)—then those reading philosophical discussions about multiculturalism might gain new insights about philosophy and multiculturalism.

Multiculturalism, as Molefi Kete Asante suggests, is pretty straightforward, perhaps explaining why people want to theorize "for it." One could do well by sticking with what Banks offers, but it is possible, I think, to be even more inclusive. Banks rightly addresses the needs of students based on the realities of social-class, racial, ethnic, and gender issues. But one could take the next step and explicitly confront homophobia and the prejudice against those who are physically challenged, thus expanding the scope of multiculturalism to unambiguously tackle all modes of unethical devaluation and social injustice in schools. In other words, multicultural education could be understood as an educational strategy that attempts to confront and challenge the obstacles and impasses that have historically presented themselves in the classroom (and outside of it) due to the unethical biases that racism, class elitism, sexism, homophobia, and other modes of prejudice impose on students and teachers. It is therefore an educational strategy that attempts to facilitate learning and teaching beyond the traditional constraints that remain in the curriculum and school structure that wrongly detract from the goal of education in a democratic and just society. Defined this way, multiculturalism could be characterized as systematically confronting all the forces at work that unfairly thwart student and teacher achievement, meaningfully combining the work of all those theoretically and pragmatically exploring and challenging traditional values and structures that function against justice—a bold program, to say the least.

Too often, however, multiculturalism is reduced solely to making ethnic minorities "feel good" about themselves and elevating any and all cultural differences to the same ethical playing field due to the relativism it allegedly promotes. There is certainly enough media coverage about all sorts of events and activities "celebrating difference," from international food festivals to world music concerts. The emphasis, even by people such as Banks in this context, is straightforwardly that cultural difference is good for everyone, a positive force in the United States and around the world. And typically what is being celebrated is at least pleasurable if not actually politically and socially transformative. Unfortunately, when limited only to promoting "celebrating difference," multiculturalism too easily allows itself to be open to the sort of criticism raised by Schlesinger, Ravitch, et al. and diminishes the positive impact of multiculturalism. It also allows for multiculturalism to be rendered obsolete once it can be demonstrated, as Nathan Glazer contends, that "we are all multiculturalists now" because we all see the value in expanding the curriculum and by being committed to "tolerance." But as sociologist Zymunt Bauman, in his book *Community: Seeking Safety in an Insecure World*, warns us with the following question,

> is cultural pluralism a value in its own right, or does its value derive from the suggestion (and hope) that it may improve the quality of shared existence? It is not immediately clear which of the two answers the multiculturalist programme prefers; the question is far from being rhetorical, and the choice between answers would

need more to be said about what is meant by the "right to difference." (p. 135)

Bauman fairly expresses his concern over the nature, structure, and implications of such pluralism in the face of globalism and other political realities that could easily manipulate the appeal for "tolerence." In the process those looking to avoid or ignore the social, cultural, and economic injustices we find around the world could point to the golden rule of multiculturalists, to respect the differences of other cultures, even if we have other values. Thus the exploitation of workers (many of them children) and the abuses of women around the world can cynically be written off as "part of that culture's history, and how dare we Eurocentrists tell them what they should do and value." Whether it is a question of what some other culture eats or who gets political representation under their system of governing, following the dictates of multiculturalism would presumably give corporations and Western economic powerhouses all the justification they would need to continue "developing" the global market and workforce.

This would be the end of multiculturalism if it were the goal and purpose to merely promote tolerating and celebrating difference. As argued above, multiculturalism is concerned with eliminating those obstacles and impasses that have been artificially imposed by the legacy of racism and sexism, among other modes of discrimination and oppression, and that continue to operate to thwart the accomplishment of students and teachers in schools across the United States. This is why multiculturalism is not just concerned with the past; new expressions of unethical devaluation and social injustices will certainly appear as the political landscape shifts. In addition, multicultural education is by definition committed to justice and ethical dialogue and thus could never accept or legitimize some culture or cultural behavior based on some universal edict that all cultures have value. Of course, all cultures do have value; part of the question is determining the nature and role of that value within the context of our democratic nation and within the course of teaching and learning. Multiculturalism has suggested that historically many cultures in the United States have had their value diminished unethically in the name of nation-building, expansion, and Christian values, and have been forced outside the political and cultural dialogue over the future of our nation even though they have contributed to the history and growth of it.

Multiculturalism demands that whatever else happens, schools in the United States must reject the residual racism that still lingers, the sexism that still undermines girls and women, the classism that still harms so many children and their parents, the homophobia that stills renders many in our democracy second-class citizens, and the institutional barriers that still pose unjust obstacles to those physically challenged trying to lead good lives and contribute to our country's well-being. The reason why multiculturalism is still a necessary educational strategy is because all of these things still exist, and multiculturalists are optimistic about the value of education and its impact on those who will lead this country in the future. Multiculturalism is still needed because it always will be needed. Contrary to Glazer's presumption that it is only the latest in a wave of educational reforms and responses, multiculturalism will never lose its relevance because it is inherently adaptable to the needs of those who wrongly suffer from discrimination. That we as a nation still have difficult questions to answer regarding the value of this or that tradition, desire, or behavior does not in any way diminish the value of multiculturalism's demand that we stop now perpetuating unethical values, antidemocratic values based on fear, prejudice, and ignorance. This is why I insist on multiculturalism *still*.

Epilogue

Teaching in an Extra-Moral Sense

to be truthful means using the customary metaphors—in moral
terms: the obligation to lie according to a fixed convention, to
lie herd-like in a style obligatory for all. . .

—Nietzsche, "On Truth and Lie in an Extra-Moral Sense"

Early in *The Republic*, Plato makes the case for introducing
lies—"fictitious stories," as he calls them—into the curriculum
of the young learners of his ideal state. Having already identified the two branches of education—the cultivation of the
mind and the body—Plato notes that it is important for those
only with the appropriate authority to "supervise the making of
fables and legends, rejecting all which are unsatisfactory"
(p. 69). The educational and moral principle put to use here is
to ensure that the young of the state, including its future leaders, are presented with only the "best" representations of the
gods and heroes and not with stories that have dangerous
faults, the kind of faults that damage the image of "noble"
things. "[M]isrepresenting the nature of gods and heroes, like
an artist whose picture is utterly unlike the object he sets out to
draw" (Ibid., p. 69), as Plato famously puts it, undermines the
moral development of the "guardian" of the state and eventually the state itself. "[H]ence the great importance of seeing
that the first stories [the guardian] hears shall be designed to

produce the best possible effect on his character" (Ibid., p. 70). The point is that all stories representing the gods and heroes of the state, but especially those told early to children, must portray the very nobility and character of what the state wishes to instill in its young. To do otherwise, by introducing stories with "faults," risks the possibility of having the young ultimately reject any loyalty to the state and having them harm their own moral character as well—or so Plato would argue.

Plato's rationale for introducing particular fictitious stories that promote desired images and censoring those that emphasize the sort of faults that would undermine the moral character of the individual, and thus the state, seems fair enough. Why would anyone challenge such an educational and political strategy? The good of both the individual and the state are being served by those in charge who are responsible for overseeing the moral development of the young. How better to perform such a duty than by *guaranteeing* the content of what the young are presented concerning the really important matters?

Plato's prescription is rather simple and straightforward; it's the narrative variant of the adage "You are what you eat"; in this case, "You are what you hear, see, etc." Perhaps more accurately stated, "You become what you are told, shown, and presented." For Plato, and every educator and psychologist since, the formative years of any child are obviously important ones, and so one must scrutinize everything the child encounters. According to Plato, the child's character formation is, in large part, developed in direct response to the "representations" she or he encounters. Thus, to inculcate a sense of piety, the stories about the gods must, in turn, generate a sense that the gods warrant such devotion. Given this formula, Plato further prescribes that

the poets *must not* tell us that "the gods go to and fro among the cities of men, disguised as strangers of all sorts from far countries"; *nor must* they tell any of those *false* tales of Proteus and Thitis transforming themselves, or bring Hera on the stage in the guise of a priestess collecting alms for "the life-giving children of Inachus, the river of Agros." Mothers, again, *are not* to follow these suggestions and scare young children with mischievous stories of spirits that go about by night in all sorts of outlandish shapes. *They would only be blaspheming the gods and at the same time making cowards of their children.* (Ibid., p. 73; emphasis added)

Instead, all stories about the gods, the state, or anything said to be noble must not be represented so as to either contradict or undermine the nobility being represented. One consequence of ignoring this proscription, in addition to others, is to raise "cowards" and not future heroes willing to fight to the death for the glory of the state.

This means, of course, censorship of one sort or another and the "manufacturing of reality," to paraphrase Noam Chomsky. The argument against such a production of images, representations, and stories is familiar to all citizens of the United States who cherish the First Amendment to the Constitution, that is, one's right to the freedom of expression—even such expression that might challenge or undermine the "nobility" of things that "best" serve the state. We have seen this drama played out, time and again, over the past few decades. From the much-heralded banning of tobacco advertisements to the more recent controversial attempts to "censor" gangsta rap music, the notion that "freedom of expression" has limits when it comes to presenting images that are considered harmful to the youth of our nation has steadily gained ground. This movement toward proscription also has produced some peculiar alliances, like the coming together of certain feminists who view all rap music as misogynistic and the religious right who are outraged by the sexually explicit language and content of many songs and videos.

Interestingly, many of those on both sides of the argument concerning values appear to ignore the full import of Plato's prescription, namely that the ethical imperative employed in the name of the state as well as of the individual is *justice*. However difficult it may be to define or implement justice, many of those involved with the ongoing debates over teaching, curriculum development, and culture wars refer to values but without a meaningful expression of justice. What often gets voiced is a passionate objection to some aspect of a given work of art or intellectual project—something is deemed morally offensive by this group or that community—but rarely is the thing in question ever considered within the larger context of justice. It seems more often than not that those decrying the moral offense are actually only angered by what they consider a violation of some prevailing convention or behavioral norm, whether it is sexual, racial, economic, or some other mode of being in the world. The main force behind these many objections appears to be little more than, "Hey, this isn't how *we* do it!" They seem to miss the crucial point that because images (representations) do in fact matter, what stories one endorses or condemns concerning our nation *must* be carefully considered, analyzed, and discussed. Instead, they engage in acts of proscription without any honest or thorough reconsideration and evaluation of their *own* stories. Too often we are left with nothing more than the demand that everyone "lie herd-like in a style obligatory for all," and the threat of violence to those who do otherwise.

Although the right has been adamant about representing American values in the curriculum, it has insisted on a history of the United States and a value system infused with the logic and limitations of primarily, if not exclusively, Anglo-Christian values. Traditionally this has meant a curriculum that emphasizes the achievements of Anglo-European and Anglo-American contributions to the creation and development of the United States. On the surface, this focus might appear to follow Plato's strategy, that the stories (histories) children hear are "designed to produce the best possible effect on [their] character" (Ibid.). But this is precisely the question and the challenge raised by multiculturalists and others: Does the traditional history effectively represent our democracy and promote the best possible effect on our students' character? Is our nation simply a creation and product of Anglo culture? To what degree does the traditional curriculum overemphasize the contributions of some Anglo-Americans and wrongly exclude or devalue the contributions of others—non-Anglos? Does not such a curriculum ultimately harm the character of students by unjustly distorting the history of our nation? James. A. Banks, Sonia Nieto, Donaldo Macedo, and others have made this point many times, yet the traditionalists still insist on *their* representation, their "fixed conventions."

In an attempt to counter the traditional representation of our nation, many in the name of multiculturalism have promoted a view of history that includes "other" stories, claiming that *every* culture has value. The argument forwarded by the proponents of this view is that a multicultural history of the United States is the representation that best ensures the ethical development of students' character. While I do agree with the view that a genuine multicultural historical perspective is pedagogically effective and just, many of those claiming to be multiculturalists are not, and what they offer is a historical, cultural, and moral relativism that the right has seized upon, criticized, and exploited. Why should the values of "every" culture be automatically accepted as equally important or good? Isn't it possible that some histories would undermine a student's commitment to social justice and democratic principles? Why should we as a nation "tolerate" practices and values that weaken our own moral vision? Too many liberals advocating "teaching tolerance" have gotten bogged down in the quagmire of "multiplicity" and "difference" and are unable to move toward articulating an ethical path out of the muck.

Both the left and the right, then, have employed Plato's prescription but have done so "using the customary metaphors" particular to their own political and moral position. The right, for example, remains "obligated" to lie according to the fixed conventions of "family values," "nationalism," and the superiority of "Christian values." The left finds itself dogmatically repeating its mantra of "diversity and tolerance" even in the face of ethical questions and conflicts emerging from embracing *all* values. Both sides, as Nietzsche suggests, have their followers "lie herd-like in a style obligatory for all." We find them employing the "customary metaphors" of either the right or the left, and in the process the truth becomes what is maintained by merely adhering to the conventions being fixed. The quest for values quickly becomes little more than the establishment and repetition of sound bites, slogans, and anthems.

Rather than rigorously thinking through the issue of values, many involved in the debate simply seek the advancement of their version of the truth. While such tenacity may typically be considered commendable in any political battle, teaching in an extra-moral sense demands something more of the participants; it requires the willingness and the ability to genuinely reconsider and reevaluate the beliefs and stories one holds dear. By no means does this suggest that nothing is worth holding on to or fighting for, but teaching in an extra-moral sense does mean transgressing the "fixed conventions" that have come to define much of our thinking, teaching, and living. To refuse such acts of transgression is to refuse the possibility of values having any meaning other than that assigned to clichés. Teaching in an extra-moral sense is, to use bell hooks' phrase, teaching to transgress.

In her book *Teaching to Transgress: Education as the Practice of Freedom*, bell hooks calls for

> renewal and rejuvenation in our teaching practices. Urging all of us to open our minds and hearts so that we can know beyond the boundaries of what is acceptable, so that we can think and rethink, so that we can create new visions, . . . celebrat[ing] teaching that enables transgression—a movement against and beyond boundaries. It is that movement which makes education the practice of freedom. (p. 12)

Teaching in an extra-moral sense is the act of such transgression, for it demands movement beyond the circumscribed domain of rectitude constructed by those using only the "customary metaphors." Teaching in an extra-moral sense is a breaking away from the "fixed conventions" that define and, in turn, restrict the freedom that ought to characterize teaching and education. Such teaching is, necessarily, risky on many levels because it does involve renewal and rejuvenation, thinking and rethinking of what we value as well as how we engage others with what we do value. For too long, teaching values has been controlled by forces at war with each other, and those who at times seem satisfied to do battle without the slightest concern for anything other than victory in the struggle over values. We have sadly settled into trench warfare in which transgression is almost impossible because the boundaries are all too fixed and everyone's energy is wasted on holding down the line. Today educators are forced to enlist and join one side or the other in the ongoing culture wars. Those who attempt to stay out of the trenches find themselves nevertheless hunkered down dodging the venomous fusillades of insults continuously being fired from both sides; remaining "neutral" is equally immobilizing.

Teaching in an extra-moral sense is an act of refusing to surrender to the stultifying effect of those championing values in the name of the "customary metaphors"; God, country, diversity, tolerance, and so on. Such teaching is an expression of open inquiry and commitment to ideas, not mere habit and blind loyalty to conventions. This kind of teaching is possible if one is willing to take certain risks and rise from the trenches, daring to move beyond the arbitrary borders established by ignorance, fear, and anger. Teaching in an extra-moral sense is possible when one is willing to risk embarrassment, resentment, exhaustion, isolation, among other personal and professional consequences. But such transgression, risk-taking, and teaching also allow for the excitement, engagement, and respect that should define education. The trouble, of course, is the spelling out of such teaching, of offering a clear and simple program or course of study for teachers to follow and learn "the method." *Teaching in an extra-moral sense, however, is not a method; it is itself a value.* Thus the preparation for such teaching cannot occur using traditional models; a different paradigm is needed.

To assert that teaching in an extra-moral sense is not a method but is itself a value is not intended to artificially or otherwise complicate and confuse matters. But admittedly it does make things more difficult. In what way, for example, is teaching in an extra-moral sense a value? How can one judge the merits of such teaching if there is no specific method or content assigned to teaching in this manner? What is there to assess? Is such an assertion just another example of the games played by those indulging in postmodern formulations? The answers to these questions are obviously important, but the way in which we approach them is also important. Many involved in education—specifically teacher preparation programs—demand "clear" objectives, methods, and outcome assessments that allow one the means to approve or disapprove a given curriculum or strategy. This is reasonable and fair, but is it enough, especially when it comes to values?

Perhaps the first question we should address is: What are values? Throughout this book I have suggested, claimed, and otherwise indicated that "values" are often an assertion of meaning and status predicated on some group's investment (emotional, political, religious) in asserting that particular meaning or status. Values, therefore, are very often a claim to some priority, desired result, or preference. For example, when someone asserts that it is "proper" to speak standard English and "wrong" to speak a nonstandard form of English, one is making a claim concerning the "status" of the difference between the two forms of English and granting priority and preference to standard English over and above the nonstandard form. The "value" being asserted is both linguistic and political, namely, that there is a claim to the superiority of standard English grammatically, semantically, and morally. But as I have tried to show, such a claim, such a value, is erroneously based on the belief that there is a legitimate claim to the "linguistic" superiority of standard English, which is at best false and at worst outright racist. In short, the value being attached to standard English is not a linguistic one but a political and aesthetic one; it is a claim for the status and meaning of standard English. Thus the "value" emanates from a given community's desire, willingness, or requirement to promote the claim of such status and meaning. Values, then, are assertions of status and meaning, not *a priori* entities that guide us to see the meaning and status of the things we encounter.

We should not see anything particularly wrong or problematic with this state of affairs. But many religious leaders, politicians, and educators would be quick to claim that this attitude represents the very sort of relativism and nihilism resulting from entertaining a postmodern view of things. I must insist, however, that they are wrong and in fact hurting their own cause, the promotion of *their* values. I say this because they persist in an effort to assert that values are something else, something other than the political, material, and aesthetic expression of "status" and "meaning." Values are therefore not empty, or necessarily bad; they are, as it were, "ethically open," that is, neither good nor bad and both good and bad, depending on the context. But whatever values are, they are simply not what many people claim them to be, namely, the ethical indices that guide one through life. Values are the articulation of what a given community takes to be its desired result, priority, or preference. This is why teaching in an extra-moral sense is itself a value, because it, too, is an assertion of meaning and status, in this case of the priority, desire, and preference to transgress and reconsider the nature of making assertions and of embracing values. In this way teaching in an extra-moral sense is different because it is a value that contains within itself the challenge to question itself; it is a "deconstructive" value, if you will, whereas most values are just the opposite, meaning resistant to internal reconsideration and examination. Unlike the articulation of some static claim to status and meaning, teaching in an extra-moral sense is dynamic and relational; its expression demands and initiates movement, transgression, even of its own status and meaning.

Let's take another example of "static" values, in particular of what some have come to call "family values," the backbone of the religious and political right in the United States. If one paid little attention to what was actually being asserted, these family values might at first sound like a set of values engaging and advancing good family living and interactions, a means toward achieving a moral and happy family. But upon closer inspection, "family values," in the context that they are asserted and advanced by those on the right, are little more than a series of fixed—that is to say, "static"—controls, rules, and preferences put forth by an orthodox community claiming universal status for their dogmatic assertions (static values). Those who have come to question these "conventions," these orthodoxies, have been boldly denounced and are considered at fault for undermining the moral foundation of our nation.

One should not assume, however, that "static" values are *ipso facto* bad or oppressive because they are static. This is not the issue; the issue is that those asserting and demanding them are doing so as if they were self-evident and obvious ethical principles, not claims made concerning the status and meaning of the conventions and practices endorsed and rigidly enforced by those who advanced them. It may very well be that most values are "static," meaning resistant to internal movement and deconstruction. This makes sense; after all, values are the assertion of status and meaning by a community regarding some convention or practice. The question is, why *must* a family be set up in the manner Rev. Jerry Falwell and the religious right claim: mother, father (read wife and husband), and children? In other words, why is one "ethically" obligated to accept their "static" values concerning family life or anything else? The fact that they assert it means nothing (ethically speaking, anyway). Why, for example, insist, as they do, that the only ethical arrangement is a traditional heterosexual partnership? Why does Rev. Falwell and his followers dismiss *prima facie* the viability and ethical efficacy of a lesbian, gay, or single-parent household? It is not so much that the value is static but that this alleged moral community has bought into it as if it were something ethical as such and something that all must agree upon. It is their myopic vision that sees a "fixed convention" as ethical imperative that is the problem. Even a cursory look at the "family values" being enforced by the right quickly reveals the fixed conventions of this group being asserted as the only practices acceptable for all, and their consequent demand "to lie herd-like in a style obligatory for all."

Of course, one should feel free to attempt to pursuade others to embrace one's own values. *Why not?* This practice seems to be part of the essence of being human, namely, trying to communicate with and influence others. Teaching in an extra-moral sense is a value attempting to do the same thing that all values do—assert itself so that others can consider it. The difference, however, between what the right (and some on the left) have been doing for a number of years and what is being suggested here is the difference between "promoting" values versus "demanding" them, and the difference between "pursuading" rather than "coercing" others to "accept" your values as worthy of their time and interest. That people want others to agree with them seems historically obvious and fairly universal; but the ways in which people strive to achieve such agreement and the consequences of such attempts are somewhat less clear and more problematic. Because of this, the relationship between accepting or rejecting values and establishing one's identity can therefore occur by default rather than by choice—*you are either one of us* or *you are not one of us*, sometimes you might be considered *one of them*, but regardless of that designation, unless you accept what we have put forth, you will always be considered *not one of us*. Understandably, for many people the desire *not to be* "one of them," and *not* "not one of us" has caused much pain, confusion, and frustration. Much of this positioning and identifying of others has happened in the name of teaching values.

Teaching in an extra-moral sense attempts, among other things, to disrupt this way of linking identity and value; it tries to reconfigure the connection between identity and value as *relational* rather than mandated by the presumption of some transcendental law and the enforcement by some morality advocate or censor. As the Swiss linguist Ferdinand de Saussure observed in his *Course in General Linguistics*, the connection between value and identity is more functional and relational rather than causal in any strict sense. As an example of such a blending of the two, de Saussure offers the following description of the identity of a chess piece and how its value is determined by its relation and function to other pieces and the game of chess itself. He tells us,

> [t]ake a knight, for instance. By itself is it an element in the game? Certainly not, for by its material make-up—outside its square and the other conditions of the game—it means nothing to the player; it becomes a real, concrete element only when endowed with value wedded to it. Suppose that the piece happens to be destroyed or lost during a game. Can it be replaced by an equivalent piece? Certainly. Not only another knight but even a figure shorn of any resemblance to a knight can be declared identical provided the same value is attributed to it. We see then that in semiological systems like language, where elements hold each other in equilibrium in accordance with fixed rules, *the notion of identity blends with that of value and vice versa.* (p. 110; emphasis added)

In a social and political context, then, the blending of identity and value is predicated on the relationship one establishes, or has imposed on, her or him by those determining "the game." This not to say that "the game" in question—let's say the setting up of a family—is not important or has no ethical issues tied to it, but that the notion of identity "blending" with that of value becomes *relational* and not causal in the fashion understood by those sponsoring a given set of values. In this case, for example, you are determined to be a good or a bad parent, child, sibbling, etc., depending on the "family values" you buy into or have imposed on you. The relationship between "good" and "bad" parent is determined by the particular "game" (family values) you find yourself agreeing to or being forced to play. One's identity (like a chess piece), therefore, is relational based on the function one performs within the game (set of values)—one either properly conforms to the structure and rules of the game or fails to do so and is accordingly identified.

Those demanding that everyone see the importance of "family values" have an ethical obligation to describe them first and then to pursuade others of their usefulness (their status and meaning). But these advocates cannot justifiably demand strict adherence to these values simply because they are the "rules of the game" established by the proponents of the game. Rules and games are not in and of themselves ethical imperatives that everyone must consider; they might be social and political facts one must negotiate in everyday life, but this hardly raises them to the status of an ethical mandate, the very sort of claim made by those espousing "family values."

Earlier on, following the thinking of bell hooks, I said that teaching in a extra-moral sense is to be understood as an act that, to use her phrase, "enables transgression," an act that encourages crossing boundaries and borders. For some, such a claim rings disingenuous, if not hollow. But even a moment's reflection demonstrates the usefulness of this "value," this assertion. As just suggested, much of what constitutes identity is the consequence of establishing and encountering boundaries and borders of one sort or another, and the relationships one enjoys or suffers as a result. In geopolitical terms this is fairly easy to "map out." For example, in what way should one come to understand the essence of being in the United States? What is the United States (or any nation, for that matter)? Certainly one could point to the Constitution, the body of laws, the Congress, etc., and this clearly matters, but for many the United States is also very much its borders, and understandably so.

Yet borders, as we have seen in recent history (the collapse of the Soviet Union, the reunification of East and West Germany, the separation of Czechoslovakia, Yugoslavia, and so on), are not fixed in any permanent manner; national lines get drawn and redrawn. The notion of establishing one's identity based on these kinds of lines of demarcation is still very powerful but tenuous nevertheless. Even within the borders of the United States, national identity changes depending on location. It matters, perhaps more for some than for others, if one is from the Northeast, the South, Alaska, Hawaii, California; one's identity is relational to the image, the terrain, the character of the region, the place that has its own boundaries within the borders of the United States. These can and often do get complicated and confusing: When does one become a New Yorker? A Minnesotan? A suburbanite? Can one occupy more than one location at a time, have more than one identity at a time, stand in relation to many things over time? How does one's identity get established?

If we consider the issue of boundaries and borders on other terms—sexual, economic, racial, as many have been doing over the years—then we see that things are even more complicated and confusing. If we include values in the mix, we can quickly make the point that the nature of one's identity to any given community, place, or time is very much relational. This does not mean that one is unidentifiable or forever in some kind of identity flux, but rather that identities are both chosen and imposed, and therefore transgressing may very well be a necessary act. It matters because of the particular history of the United States, whether one is identified as black, biracial, white, gay, bisexual, spiritual, or religious, and it matters who does the identifying.

Transgressing boundaries and borders of these sorts is not to be confused with the mere act of "crossing over" some line or gateway, although even crossing over can prove wonderful or deadly. The movement involved with transgressing is not a movement to subsume or consume something other, someone other. It is an act of freedom, of exploring and understanding. Teaching in an extra-moral sense attempts to support this movement, this freedom. It is an assertion of the status and meaning of such freedom; this is why it, too, is a value. Teaching in an extra-moral sense understands education in the context of all of those who have struggled to liberate education from those who want to stop such transgressing and impose strict boundaries and borders. Teaching in an extra-moral sense challenges those teaching values as a means to shut down pathways in and out of domains of thinking and living.

The paradigm of such teaching has been laid out before us; it is dialogue. Teaching in an extra-moral sense is genuine dialogue, the movement between and among those thinking, teaching, learning, and living in the world. This is why so many have begun and continue to teach in an extra-moral sense; they have already understood and promoted dialogue as the means to critical consciousness, as the way to move intellectually, politically, and ethically. Paulo Friere, bell hooks, Henry Giroux, Peter McLaren, Jonathan Kozol, Sonia Neito, James A. Banks, and so many others have advocated dialogue in different ways and settings for so long, yet the resistance to such movement is just as real. So part of teaching in an extra-moral sense has necessarily been teaching beyond that resistance, teaching against the boundaries and borders of racism, sexism, homophobia, class elitism, teaching beyond the boundaries and borders of the "customary metaphors" and "fixed conventions."

Teaching in an extra-moral sense is teaching within the context of multiculturalism and postmodernism, but it is also teaching within the context of the history of learning itself. Teaching in an extra-moral sense is not a new, or even a modern phenomenon; it is what real teaching has always been. The question is whether enough educators have the courage, strength, and knowledge to continue risking moving on, beyond the limits of the political forces at work, busy teaching values. If there are, then teaching will continue to be a process of facilitating learning, of supporting movement from one place to another, from ignorance to knowledge, from hate to understanding, from indifference to caring.

Bibliography

Asante, M. K. "Multiculturalism: An Exchange." In *Debating P. C.: The Controversy over Political Correctness on College Campuses*, edited by P. Berman. New York: Dell, 1992.

———. *Malcolm X as Cultural Hero and Other Afrocentric Essays*, Trenton, N.J.: Africa World Press. 1993.

Bachelard, G. *The Poetics of Space*, Boston: Beacon Press. 1969.

Baldwin, J. "If Black Isn't a Language, Then Tell Me, What Is It?" In *The Real Ebonics Debate: Power, Language, and the Education of African-American Children*, edited by T. Perry and L. Delpit. Boston: Beacon Press, 1998.

Banks, J. A. *An Introduction to Multicultural Education*, Boston: Allyn and Bacon. 1999.

Baraka, A. (a.k.a. L. Jones). *Blues People: The Negro Experience in White America and the Music That Developed from It*. New York: William Morrow, 1963.

Bauman, Z. *Community: Seeking Safety in an Insecure World*. London: Polity, 2000.

Bennett, W. *The Devaluing of America: The Fight for Our Culture and Our Children*. New York: Summit Books, 1992.

Boal, A. *Theatre of the Oppressed*. New York: Theatre Communications Group, 1985.

———. *Games for Actors and Non-Actors*. New York: Routledge, 1992.

Bordo, S. *Twilight Zones: The Hidden Life of Cultural Images from Plato to O. J.* Berkeley: University of California Press, 1997.

Bryson, B. *The Mother Tongue: English and How It Got That Way.* New York: Avon Books, 1990.

Butler, J. *Gender Trouble: Feminism and the Subversion of Identity.* New York: Routledge, 1990.

———. *Bodies that Matter: On the Discursive Limits of "Sex."* New York: Routledge, 1993.

———. *The Psychic Life of Power: Theories in Subjection.* Stanford Calif.: Stanford University Press, 1997.

Casey, E. S. *Getting Back into Place: Toward a Renewed Understanding of the Place-World,* Bloomington: Indiana University Press, 1993.

Cornford, F. M. *Before and after Socrates.* London: Cambridge University Press, 1974.

Crystal, D. "The Prescriptive Tradition." In *Language Awarness,* edited by P. Escholy, et. al. Boston: St. Martin's Press, 2000.

Danticat, E. *Breath, Eyes, and Memory.* New York: Vintage Contemporary Editions, 1995.

de Saussure, F. *Course in General Linguistics,* New York: McGraw-Hill, 1966.

Donne, J. "An Anatomy of the World." In *The Complete Poetry and Selected Prose of John Donne and William Blake,* compiled by R. S. Hillyer. New York: Modern Library, 1941.

D'Souza, D. *Illiberal Education: The Politics of Race and Sex on Campus.* New York: The Free Press, 1991.

Ehrenreich, B. "The Challenge for the Left." In *Debating P.C.: The Controversy over Political Correctness on College Campuses,* edited by Paul Bernman. New York: Dell Publishing, 1992.

Emerson, R. W. "Nature." In *The Portable Emerson,* edited by C. Bode. New York: Penguin Books, 1983.

Foucault, M. "On the Geneology of Ethics: An Overview of Works in Progress." In *The Foucault Reader,* edited by P. Rabinow and H. Drafus. New York: Pantheon, 1984.

———. "The Concern for Truth." In *Michel Foucault: Politics, Philosophy Culture,* edited by L. D. Kritzman. New York: Routledge, 1988.

Freire, P. *Pedagogy of the Oppressed.* New York: Continuum, 1992.

Freire, P., and A. Faundez. *Learning to Question: A Pedagogy of Liberation.* New York: Continuum, 1989.

Fuss, D. *Essentially Speaking: Feminism, Nature, and Difference*. New York: Routledge, 1989.

Giroux, H. "Living Dangerously: Identity Politics and the New Cultural Racism." In *Between Borders: Pedagogy and the Politics of Cultural Studies*, edited by H. Giroux and P. McLaren. New York: Routledge, 1994.

Glazer, N. *We Are All Multiculturalists Now*. Cambridge, Mass.: Harvard University Press, 1997.

Gutmann, A., ed. *Multiculturalism: Examining the Politics of Recognition*. Princeton, N.J.: Princeton University Press, 1997.

Herron, C. *Nappy Hair*. New York: Alfred A. Knopf, Dragonfly Books, 1997.

Hirsch, E. D. Jr. *Cultural Literacy: What Every American Needs to Know*. New York: Vintage Books, 1988.

Holy Bible. King James Version. New York: New American Library, 1974.

hooks, b. *Talking Back: Thinking Feminist/Thinking Black*. Boston: South End Press, 1989.

———. *Black Looks: Race and Representation*. Boston: South End Press, 1992.

———. *Teaching to Transgress: Education as the Practice of Freedom*. New York: Routledge, 1994.

———. *Happy to Be Nappy*. New York: Hyperion Books for Children, 1999.

Jackson, S., and J. Jordan. *I've Got a Story to Tell: Identity and Place in the Academy*. New York: Peter Lang, 1999.

James, W. "Pragmatism's Conception of Truth." In *The Writings of William James: A Comprehensive Edition*, edited by J. J. McDermott, 1998. New York: Modern Library, 1968.

Kimball, R. *Tenured Radicals: How Politics Has Corrupted Our Higher Education*. Chicago: Ivan R. Dee, Elephant Paperbacks, 1998.

Kohl, H. *I Won't Learn from You*. New York: The New Press, 1999.

Kozol, J. *Savage Inequalities: Children in America's Schools*. New York: Crown, 1991.

———. *Amazing Grace: The Lives of Children and the Conscience of a Nation*. New York: HarperCollins, 1996.

Lakoff, R. T. *Talking Power: The Politics of Language*. New York: Basic Books, 1990.

Maurrasse, D. J. *Beyond the Campus: How Colleges and Universities Form Partnerships with Their Communities.* New York: Routledge, 2001.

Macedo, D. *Literacies of Power: What Americans Are Not Allowed to Know.* Boulder, Colo.: Westview Press, 1994.

McLaren, P. *Critical Pedagogy and Predatory Culture: Oppositional Politics in a Postmodern Era.* New York: Routledge, 1995.

Mohanty, C. T. " On Race and Voice." In *Between Borders: Pedagogy and the Politics of Cultural Studies,* edited by H. Giroux and P. McLaren. New York: Routledge, 1994.

Morrison, T., ed. *Race-ing Justice, En-gendering Power,* New York: Pantheon Books, 1992.

Nelson, G. *HipHop America.* New York: Penguin, 1998.

Nelson, J. *Straight No Caser: How I Became a Grown-up Black Woman.* New York: Penguin, 1999.

Newman, L. *Heather Has Two Mommies.* Los Angeles: Alyson, 2000.

Nieto, S. *Affirming Diversity: The Sociopolitical Context of Multicultural Education.* White Plains, N.Y.: Longman, 1996.

Nietzsche, F. *On the Genealogy of Morals,* edited by W. Kaufmann. New York: Vintage, 1969.

———. "On Truth and Lie in an Extra-Moral Sense." In *The Portable Nietzsche,* edited by W. Kaufmann. New York: Penguin, 1980.

Palmer, P. J. *The Courage to Teach: Exploring the Inner Landscape of a Teacher's Life.* San Francisco: Jossey-Bass, 1998.

Perry, T., and L. Delpit. eds. *The Real Ebonics Debate: Power, Language, and the Education of African-American Children.* Boston: Beacon Press, 1998.

Plato. "Apology." In *Plato: The Collected Dialogues,* edited by E. Hamilton and H. Cairns. Princeton, N.J.: Princeton University Press, 1961.

———. "Republic." In *The Republic of Plato,* translated and edited by F. M. Cornford. London: Oxford University Press, 1979.

———. "Euthyphro." In *Euthyphro, Apology, Crito,* translated by F. J. Church trans. Indianapolis: Bobbs-Merrill Education, 1980.

Ravitch, D. "Multiculturalism: E Pluribus Plures." In *Debating P.C.: The Controversy over Political Correctness on College Campuses,* edited by P. Berman. New York: Dell, 1992.

Saltman, K. J. *Collateral Damage: Corporatizing Public Schools—A Threat to Democracy.* Lanham, Md.: Rowman and Littlefield, 2000.

Schlesinger A., Jr. *The Disuniting of America: Reflections on a Multicultural Society.* New York: W. W. Norton, 1993.

Smith, B. H. "Cult-Lit: Hirsch, Literacy, and National Culture." In *The Politics of Liberal Education,* edited by D. J. Gless and B. H. Smith. Durham, N.C.: Duke University Press, 1992.

Sokal, A. "Transgressing the Boundaries: Toward a Transformative Hermeneutics of Quantum Gravity." *Social Text* 46 (1997): 47.

West, C. "Diverse New World." In *Debating P.C.: The Controversy over Political Correctness on College Campuses,* edited by Paul Bernman. New York: Dell, 1992.

———. *Beyond Eurocentrism and Multiculturalism.* Vol. 1: *Prophetic Thought in Postmodern Times.* Monroe, Maine: Common Courage Press, 1993.

———. *Race Matters.* New York: Vintage Books, 1994.

Willett, C. 1998. *Theorizing Multiculturalism: A Guide to the Current Debate.* London: Blackwell, 1998.

Index

academic achievement, 140
academic elitism, 126
Académie française, 81, 86
Accademia della Crusca, 80
actor, 128–129
acts of repetition, 125, 130
aesthetic revolution, 32
aesthetic values. *See* beauty
*Affirming Diversity: The
    Sociopolitical Context of
    Multicultural Education*
    (Nieto), 84, 142
Africa, 59
African(s), 30
    costumes, 138
    languages, 73, 74
    names, 138
    rituals, 138
African-American, 29, 37, 41,
    51, 52–53, 56, 74–77,
    86–87, 96, 115, 135. *See
    also* blacks
    community, 41, 53
    culture, 77, 87
    language, 74–75, 86
    multiculturalism and, 135
    students, 77, 96, 115
Afrocentrists, 137, 141–142
age of uncertainty, 9, 34, 37–39
    discomfort from, 37

living in, 37
    teaching in, 37–39
ageism, 100
Alfred A. Knopf Publishers, 54
Algeria, 73
alienation, 66–67
America
    bleaching of, 81
American(s), 1–2, 20–21, 37, 72,
    74, 134–137, 140, 142, 147,
    164
    black, 138
    culture, 72, 134–136, 140
    history, 137, 142, 164
    students, 142, 147
    teachers, 142
    values, 1–2, 20–21, 37, 164
*An Introduction to Multicultural
    Education* (Banks), 142
Anglo-American contributions,
    165
Anglocentric culture, 136
Anglo-Christian values, 164
Anglo-European influences,
    139, 165
anti-Semitism, 46–47
Apology (Plato), 70
Appiah, K. Anthony, 155
Arabic, 73
Archimedes, 89

Asante, Kete Molefi, 82, 83–84,
    141–142, 156
Asian-Americans, 96

Babel, 70
Bachelard, Gaston, 99
Baktin, M.M., 78
Baldwin, James, 75–76, 86, 89,
    96
Banks, James, A., 15, 142,
    143–152, 156–157, 165, 176
Baraka, Amiri, 74, 86
Bauman, Zymunt, 157–158
beauty, 48–49, 59–60, 63–64
Before and after Socrates
    (Cornford), 35
being, 111
beliefs, 33
Bennett, William, 1–2, 9,
    20–22, 24, 28, 34, 98, 143
*Beyond the Campus: How Colleges
    and Universities Form
    Partnerships with Their
    Communities* (Maurrasse), 105
Bible, 70, 75
bilingual education, 65, 67, 85
black(s), 29, 37, 49, 51, 52, 56,
    60–62, 75, 114, 138. *See
    also* African-American
    Americans, 138
    children, 49
    church, 75
    diaspora, 75
    pride, 60–62
Black English, 12, 15, 62–63,
    65–66, 75–77, 84–87. *See
    also Ebonics*
    debate on, 77
    in schools, 77
    speakers of, 77
    subordination of, 77
    value of, 85
bleaching of America, 81
Bloom, Harold, 78
Blues People: The Negro

*Experience in White American
    and the Music That Developed
    from It* (Baraka), 74
Boal, Augusto, 14, 128–130
Book of Genesis, 70
Bordo, Susan, 48
Bowen, Barbara, 91
Braggs, Kingsley, 113–115
Brazil, 73
Breath, Eyes and Memory
    (Dantiat), 108
British, 84
Bronx, the, 93, 95
Brooklyn, 41
Bryson, Bill, 78–79, 83
Burchfield, 78–79
Butler, Judith, 14, 110–112, 114,
    119, 124, 127, 129

call and response, 54–55, 61
Canada, 73
capitalist, 63
Cardinal Richelieu, 80
Cartesian coordinates, 148
Casey, Edward, 104
Catholic institution, 93, 96
"Caught in the Cross-Fire: A
    young star teacher finds
    herself in a losing racial battle
    with parents" (Clemetson
    article), 45
celebrating difference, 158
censorship, 162–163
Central Park, 94–95
Cepeda, Joe, 54
character formation, 162, 165
chess piece, 173–174
Chinese culture, 148
choices, 120
Chomsky, Noam, 163
Christian values, 159
citizenship, 139
City College of New York
    (CUNY), 46, 90, 98, 143
City University of New York, 46

civil rights movement, 144
class, 118, 126
class elitism, 38, 100, 176
classroom, 65–66, 116, 118, 125, 128, 131
  control, 116
  discipline, 116
  management, 116
  performance, 116, 118, 120
Clemetson, Lynette, 45, 49
Clinton, William, 72
Collateral Damage: Corporatizing Public Schools—A Threat to Democracy (Saltman), 116–117
College of Mount Saint Vincent, 7, 90, 92, 94, 97–98, 100–108, 133
Columbia University, 51–52
Columbus, Christopher, 28
communication
  pragmatics of, 82–83, 85
Community: Seeking Safety in an Insecure World (Bauman), 157
"Concern for Truth" (Foucault interview), 24–25
conscientization, 128
conservative. *See* political right
content integration, 144–146, 148
Continental philosophy, 8
Cornford, F. M., 36
corporations, 158
cosmos, 147
counterrevolution, 136
courage, 37, 39
Courage to Teach, The (Palmer), 39
Course in General Linguistics (de Saussure), 172–173
cowards, 163
critical pedagogy, 33, 123
Critical Pedagogy and Predatory Culture (McLaren), 33–34
critical perspectives, 6, 8–9, 14, 23

argument and, 23
  education and, 6, 8–9, 14
critical race theory, 122
cross-cultural confusions, 46
cross-cultural interactions, 42, 44, 52
Crystal, David, 80
cult, 136
"Cult-Lit: Hirsch, Literacy, and the National Culture" (Smith essay), 26–27
cultural assumptions, 149
cultural conquest, 73
cultural differences, 157
cultural diversity, 1, 51
cultural genes, 140
cultural information, 145
cultural injustices, 158
cultural literacy, 26
Cultural Literacy (Hirsch), 25–26
cultural pluralism, 157–158
cultural relativism, 20, 26, 165
cultural space, 123
cultural transformation, 37
culture
  African-American, 77
  American, 72, 134–136, 140
  ancient, 147
  Anglocentric, 136
  Chinese, 148
  common, 140
  dominant, 123
  Egyptian, 148
  ethnic, 135
  Greek, 147–148
  school, 152
  value of, 158–159
  Western, 144
culture wars, 44–45, 99, 134–135, 164, 167
curiosity, 35
curriculum
  development, 164
  dumbing down, 151
  multicultural, 146

curriculum *(continued)*
   Plato's, 161
   value-centered, 99

Danticat, Edwidge, 108
Dasey, Edward S., 89
Davis, Ron, 51
debate
   Black English, 77
   English usage, 65–69
   between left and right, 166
   medicine, 148
   on multiculturalism, 142–143
   national, 44
   philosophical, 154
   standard English, 78, 169
   television, 143
   values, 1–5, 22
deconstructionism, 5, 37. *See
   also* postmodernism
Deleuze, Gilles, 129
Delpit, Lisa, 76
demagogues, 137
de-mechanization, 128–130
democracy, 11–12, 20, 26–27,
   34, 37, 68, 72, 85, 138, 165
   challenge to, 34
   future of, 26
   language and, 72
   shared knowledge and, 26–27
   traditional history and, 165
   truth and, 37
   undermining of, 85
"Democracy in a Different
   Voice" (Media Education
   Foundation), 112
democratic dialogue, 128
democratic impulse, 34
Democratic Left (West), 23–24
democratic principles, 152, 165
democratic system, 159
Derrida, Jacques, 6, 21, 78
deSaussure, Ferdinand, 172–173
De-Valuing of America (Bennett),
   21, 28–30

Dewey, John, 32
Dinkins, David, 98
discipline, 116
discrimination, 159
discursively constituted identity,
   110, 112, 118, 127
*Disuniting of America: Reflections
   on a Multicultural Society, The*
   (Schlesinger), 136
doctors, 148
doer, 111
dogmatism, 3
dominant culture, 123
dominant regimes, 123
Donne, John, 19
Dragonfly Books, 54
Dryfus, Herbert, 120
D'Sousa, Dinesh, 10, 20, 22–24,
   34, 143
Dutch, 73

Eagleton, Terry, 78
"Eating the Other: Desire and
   Resistance" (hooks essay), 122
ebonics, 15, 77. *See also* Black
   English
economic injustices, 158
education
   American, 24, 131, 134
   banking concept of, 127–128
   bilingual, 65, 67, 85
   critical perspectives, 6, 8–9, 14
   democracy and, 10–11
   evaluation of, 116
   extra-moral, 9
   institutions, 121
   interdisciplinary, 93
   leadership, 7
   liberal, 23
   multicultural, 10–11, 92, 98–99
   myths and lies in, 27–28
   observation of, 116
   performative dynamics, 116,
      121, 130–131
   place in, 13, 89, 96, 99–101

policy, 5, 7
policymaking for, 3–4
politics of, 134
prejudice in, 7–8
prescription for, 4
progress, 44
purpose of, 128
reform movement, 153, 156
strategies, 69, 138
urban, 13, 42, 65, 92, 98–99
values-centered, 23
educators, 14, 17, 20, 56,
   116–118, 127–128, 145
American, 35
evaluation of, 117
knowledge of, 117
men and women of color as,
   118
performance of, 117–119
power and, 127
progressive, 128
transgressive, 128
urban, 92
Egyptian culture, 148
Ehrenreich, Barbara, 21
elitism, 28, 126
Emerson, Ralph Waldo, 31–32,
   33
eminent domain, 95
England, 84
English
   Black, 12, 15, 62–63, 65–66,
      75–77, 85–87
   grammar, 78
   king's, 60
   language, 66, 84
   nonstandard, 11–12, 65–69,
      72–73, 76–77, 87, 169
   queen's, 60
   rules and regulations, 79
   standard, 11–12, 60, 65–69,
      72–73, 75, 84, 87, 169
   substandard, 11–12, 66, 85, 87
English Language (Burchfield), 79
Enlightenment, 20

Epicenter for the Study of Oral
   Poetry at Harvard, 52
epistemology, 126
epithet, 53
equality, 112
equity pedagogy, 151
"Essentialism in the Classroom"
   (Fuss), 126
ethical action, 69
ethical dialogue, 158
ethical imperative, 127, 164, 171
ethical person, 120
ethnic culture, 135
ethnic minorities, 157
ethnic tension, 143
ethnic uniqueness, 51
ethnicity, 122–123
ethnocentric curricula, 30
Eurocentric values, 2, 25,
   140–141
Eurocentrists, 158
"Euthyphro" (Plato dialogue),
   35–36
Ewald, François, 24
exploitation, 158
extra-moral teaching, 15,
   166–168, 170, 172, 174, 176
extra-moral values, 15

fables, 161
Falwell, Jerry, 1–2, 20, 171
family values, 2, 38, 166
Faundes, Antonio, 35
feminism, 122, 153
feminists, 25, 163
Fernandez, Joseph, 97
Florida voting debacle, 72
Fonthill Castle, 95
foreign language, 85
Forrest, Edwin, 95
Foucault, Michel, 6, 14, 24,
   120–122, 124, 128, 149
France, 80
freedom of expression, 163
Freire, Paolo, 37, 127–128, 176

French, 73, 86
Freud, Sigmund, 149
Fuss, Diana, 126

Games for Actors and non-Actors
   (Boal), 128
gangsta rap music, 163
Gap, The, 85
gays, 37, 171
gaze, 114
   affectionate, 114–115
   interrogation of, 114, 115
   oppositional, 114
gender, 14, 110–112, 118, 123
   historical context and, 110
   identity, 111
   studies, 123
Gender Trouble (Butler), 110
Genesis, 70–71
gentlemen, 112, 115, 122
German immigrants, 95
Getting Back into Place (Casey),
   89
Giroux, Henry, A., 6, 14, 123,
   124, 129, 131, 176
Giuliani, Rudolph, 98
Glazer, Nathan, 15, 133–137,
   140–144, 157, 159
global market, 158
global workforce, 158
globalism, 158
God, 59–60, 62–64, 70–71
gods, 161–162
Graduate Program in Urban
   and Multicultural Education,
   90, 102, 133
grammarians, 78
Greek, 91, 147–148
   culture, 147–148
   mathematicians, 147
Guiner, Lani, 112, 114
Gutmann, Amy, 154–155

Habermas, Jürgen, 155
habit, 112

Happy to Be Nappy (hooks), 63–64
Harding, Sandra, 149
Harrington, Michael, 91
Harvard, 52
Heather Has Two Mommies
   (Newman), 97
Hegel, G.W. F., 78
Heidegger Martin, 78
heroes, 161–163
Herring, Dennis, L., 52
Herron, Carolivia, 41, 49, 57,
   60, 62
heterosexual privilege, 110
hip-hop, 85
Hirsch, E.D., Jr., 25–27
   literacy list of, 26–27, 37
Hispanic community, 41
Hispanics, 37, 52, 96
historical relativism, 165
history
   abuse of, 137
   alternative, 138
   complexity of, 138
   corruption of, 138
   purpose of, 137
   of science, 146–147
   as therapy, 138
   undoing, 137
   United States, 137, 142,
      164–165, 175
   as weapon, 137
Holloway, Lynette, 50
homophobia, 8, 100, 151, 156,
   159, 176
hooks, bell, 6, 14, 37, 63, 78,
   114–115, 122, 124, 128–129,
   166, 174, 176
Hudson River Valley, 95
human freedom, 127–128
human language, 130
Hyperion Books for Children, 63

identity, 30, 33, 37, 75, 109–112,
   118, 123–127, 139, 151,
   153, 172

black, 30, 37
    construction of, 124
    cultural, 33
    discursively constituted, 110, 112, 118, 127
    gender, 111
    moral, 33
    national, 33, 75, 139
    politics, 126, 153
    racial, 151
    sexual, 109
    simple acts and, 112, 125–126
    singular, 123
    value and, 172
Illiberal Education (D'Sousa), 22–23
India, 73
information
    selectivity of, 28
    shared, 26–28
instructors. *See* educators
integrity, 37, 39
intellectual transformation, 32, 37
intercultural communication, 141
international food festivals, 157
intersubjectivity, 23–24
intolerance, 7–8, 23
Irish immigrants, 95
irrational numbers, 147
Italy, 80
I've Got a Story to Tell: Identity and Place in the Academy (Jackson & Jordan), 118

Jackson, Sandra, 118, 122
James, William, 32
Jefferson Airplane, 19
Jeffries, Leonard, 46–47, 98, 143
Johnson, Kevin J., 71
Jones, LeRoi. *See* Baraka, Amiri
Jordan, Jose Solis, 118, 122
Judeo-Christian values, 2, 38
justice, 22, 40, 164

Kimball, Roger, 20
knowledge, 117
knowledge construction process, 148–149
Kohl, Herbert, 29–31
Kozol, Jonathan, 40, 176
Kramer, Hilton, 20
Kruger, Steve, 91
Ku Klux Klan, 113
Kwanza, 77

La Bourgeois Gentilhomme (Molière), 130
Lakoff, Robin Tolmach, 69
language, 11–12, 69, 72–77, 81, 83–86, 130
    adoption of, 73
    African, 73
    African-American, 74–75, 86
    codification of, 81
    corporate valuation of, 85
    correctness, 83
    diversity of, 85
    dynamics of, 77, 84
    enforcement of, 81
    foreign, 85
    human, 130
    native, 85
    nature of, 72
    oppression and, 72–73
    origin of, 75–76
    politics and, 11–12, 69
    of postmodernism, 5–6
    regulation of, 81
    sexually explicit, 163
    survival and, 70–71
    theatrical, 130
    usage, 83–84
language arts, 144
Language Awareness (Escholy), 80
Latin, 78, 91
law professor, 112, 114, 122
Learning to Question: A Pedagogy of Liberation (Faundez), 35

legends, 161
lesbians, 37, 171
lesson plan, 116–118
liberal, 130, 166
liberal education, 23
life, 129
Lingua Franca, 150
*Literacies of Power: What
　Americans Are Not Allowed to
　Know* (Macedo), 27–28, 81
literacy
　American, 26–27
　cultural, 26
"Living Dangerously: Identity
　Politics and the New Cultural
　Racism" (Giroux), 123
love, 37, 39, 40, 63
loyalty, 162

Macedo, Donaldo, 6, 27–29, 81,
　137, 165
*Malcom X as Culture Hero and
　Other Afrocentric Essays*
　(Asante), 82
Manhattan, 103
manufacturing of reality, 163
Maurrasse, David J., 105–106
Mayan civilization, 71
McDonald's, 85
McGown's Pass, 94
McLaren, Peter, 6, 31, 34
Media
　images, 49
　news, 10, 41–42, 45, 62, 143
Mexico, 73
minority children, 140
misogynistic rap music, 163
misrepresentation, 161
Modrys, Walter, 113
Mohanty, Chandra Talpace, 125
Molière, 130
Mongolia, 74
Mongolian, 74
monkey, 113, 115, 122
Monsieur Jourdain, 130

moral character, 162
moral development, 161–162
moral guidance, 37
moral imperative, 68–69
moral judgments, 21
moral offense, 163
moral relativism, 165
moral values, 69
morality, 3
Morocco, 73
Morrison, Toni, 44
*Mother Tongue: English and How
　It Got That Way, The*
　(Bryson), 78
Mount Saint Vincent. *See*
　College of Mount Saint
　Vincent
multicultural curriculum, 97
multicultural education, 10–11,
　14–15, 54, 92, 98–99, 143–159
　content integration, 144–146,
　　148
　dimensions of, 144–153
　problems in, 15
　responsibility in, 149
　social justice through, 15
multiculturalism, 14, 99,
　133–159
　balkanization and, 135
　confusion over, 154
　debate over, 142–143
　definition of, 156–157
　distortion of, 142
　divisiveness of, 135
　in education, 134
　end of, 158
　ethnic upsurge and, 137
　extreme, 139–140
　false splitting of, 142–143
　friendly confusion over,
　　154–155
　global perspective and, 144
　knowledge construction
　　process and, 148–149
　language arts and, 144

movement, 143–144
particularistic, 140–141
philosophical analysis and, 154–155
pluralistic, 140–141
politics of, 155
prejudice reduction and, 150–151
price of, 135
restriction of, 145
social studies and, 144
solidarity through, 136
v. tolerance, 15, 157
v. Western culture, 144
"Multiculturalism: An Exchange" (Asante), 141
"Multiculturalism: E Pluribus Plures" (Ravitch), 139
Multiculturalism: Examining the Politics of Recognition (Gutmann), 154–155
multiracial society, 22
myth
African, 74
education, 27–29
political right, 17
of simple act, 112
U.S. history, 30, 138

Nappy Hair (Herron), 10–11, 41–64
complexity of, 55–60
critique of, 51
narrative structure, 55–58
national identity, 139, 174–175
Anglo-European influence on, 139
non-Anglo influence on, 139
nationhood, 139
Native Americans, 37
native language, 85
Nelson, Jill, 52
New Jersey, 95
New Mexico, 59
New York City, 94, 98

New York City Board of Education, 46
New York City Teacher Center, 101–102
New York Daily News, 113
New York Post, 42, 43, 46–47, 49–50
New York State Legislature, 95
New York Times, 50–52, 71, 75
New York University, 150
Newsweek, 45–49
Nia, Isoke, T., 51–52, 56
Nieto, Sonia, 84, 142, 165, 176
Nietzsche, Friedrich Wilhelm, 15, 111, 149, 161, 166
nihilism, 20
non-Euclidean geometry, 148
nonstandard English, 11–12, 65, 67, 72–74, 76–77, 84–85, 87, 169
benefits of, 74
handicap of, 84–85
value of, 77
non-whites, 44
Norman Conquest, 86
North America, 84
"Nun in Racial Flap" (Daily News), 113

Oakland School Board, 77
objectivity, 23
O'Brien, Anthony, 91
Ohio State University, 71
"On Race and Voice" (Mohanty essay), 125
"On the Genealogy of Ethics: An overview of Works in Progress" (Foucault), 120
On the Genealogy of Morals (Nietzsche), 111
On Truth and Lie in an Extra-moral Sense (Nietzsche), 161
ontology, 126
"Oppositional Gaze, The" (hooks essay), 114

Palisades cliffs, 95
Palmer, Parker, J., 39
particularistic multiculturalism,
    140–141
particularists, 140
patriarchy, 63
patronizing, 66–67
"Paulo Freire" (West
    commentary), 127
pedagogical problem, 54
pedagogy, 33, 68–69, 73,
    118–119, 123, 151
  bad, 69
  critical, 33, 123
  equity, 151
  representational, 123
Pedagogy of the Oppressed
    (Freire), 127
Peirce, Charles, S., 32
people of color, 127
performative dynamics, 116, 121
  reevaluation of, 121
  shared context of, 121
  of teaching, 130–131
  techniques of, 121
permanent resident, 75
Perry, Theresa, 76
Peyser, Andrea, 43, 46–47, 49
phalocentrism, 25
philosophical analysis, 156
philosophy, 8
Pilgrims, 28
place in education, 13, 89, 96,
    99–101
Plato, 35–36, 70, 78, 149,
    161–163, 165–166
pluralistic multiculturalism,
    140–141
pluralists, 140
Poetics of Space (Bachelard), 99
polio vaccine, 91
political conquest, 73
political correctness, 44–46, 94
political left, 2, 5, 17, 21, 166
  value vacuum, 7

political right, 2, 5, 16–17, 21,
    34, 37, 137, 166, 170. *See also*
    religious right
  intolerance of, 2
  mythology of, 17
political transformation, 37
politics, 10–12, 22, 69, 72, 123,
    126, 134
  knowledge and, 22
  language and, 11–12
  power and, 69–72
Polynesian navigation, 148
Portuguese, 73
postmodernism, 1, 5, 9–10, 17,
    20–23, 29, 35, 37, 150, 169.
    See also deconstructionism;
    political left
  absurdity of, 150
  American values and, 22, 26,
    34
  cynicism of, 6
  distrust of, 22
  language of, 5–6
  logic of, 5–6
  nihilism of, 169
  pragmatism and, 33
  questioning by, 35, 37
  relativism of, 21, 26, 169
  teaching within, 9–10
postmodernists, 35, 153
power, 22–23, 48, 69–73, 77
  female, 48
  language and, 69–73
  politics and, 69–71
  rationing of, 22
pragmatism, 32–33
  postmodernism and, 32–33
"Pragmatism's Conception of
    Truth" (James essay), 32–33
pre-Columbian America, 71
prejudice
  in education, 7–8
  freedom from, 37
  of physically challenged, 156,
    159

racial, 45
reduction, 150–151
prescriptivism, 80, 82
present participle, 79
pride, 60–63, 120
  black, 60–63
privilege, 2, 14, 22, 110, 116,
  119–121
  acts of, 110, 119–122
  heterosexual, 110
  other side of, 121
  social, 22
professor, 118–119, 125
prolife, 2
pronunciation, 84
proscription, 163–164
Proteus, 163
public education, 117

Québec Province, 73
Queens College, 90–92, 104
queer theory, 91, 153
questioning, 34–37, 38–40,
  122
  resistance toward, 37
  Socratic, 35–36

Rabinow, Paul, 120
race, 118, 123
race memory, 140
*Race-ing, Justice, En-gendering
  Power* (Morrison), 44
racial attitudes, 150–151
racial identity, 151
racial tension, 143
racism, 10, 37, 41–42, 44, 64,
  100, 102, 113, 123, 126, 135,
  159, 176. *See also* prejudice
racist, 139
Rainbow Curriculum, 97
Ravitch, Diane, 15, 98,
  139–141, 143–144, 151, 157
Reading and Writing Project,
  51–52
reading comprehension, 57–58

*Real Ebonics Debate: Power,
  Language, and the Education of
  African-American Children*
  (Perry & Delpit), 76–77
real practices, 120
recruitment, 97
regimes of representation, 123,
  129
religious right, 2, 5, 17, 21, 34,
  37, 163, 170
representations, 161–162,
  164–165
Republic, The (Plato), 161–162
Republican Party, 72
rights, 22
Robertson, Pat, 20

Salk, Jonas, 91
Saltman, Kenneth J., 116
Santiago, Felicita, 41–42
Schlesinger , Arthur, Jr., 15,
  136–138, 140–141, 143–144,
  151, 157
school(s)
  American, 28, 159
  culture, 152
  structure, 152
School of Education at Queens
  College (CUNY), 90
"School Officials Support
  Teacher on Book That
  Parents Call Racially
  Insensitive" (Holloway
  article), 50
science
  history of, 146–147
  non-Western, 147
  teachers, 146–147
  teaching of, 148
  Western, 147
scientific methodology, 148
scientific research, 147
segregation, 97
self, 118, 120–122, 130
  formation of, 120

self *(continued)*
   reformed, 121
   techniques of, 120–122, 130
self-analysis, 122
self-awareness, 58
self-esteem, 44, 46, 49, 53–54,
   57–58, 64, 140
self-hatred, 53–54, 57, 61
Seneca Village, 95
Seton, Sister Mary, 113, 114
sex appeal, 48
sexism, 8, 10, 37, 42, 44, 46, 48,
   100, 126, 176
sexual identity, 109
Sexuality, 109. *See also* Gender
sexualizing women, 48
sexually explicit language, 163
Shakespeare, William, 83
shame, 59–60
Sherman, Ruth, 10–11, 41–54,
   62
simple acts, 112–114, 116,
   119–128, 130–131
   disruption of, 125, 130–131
   interrogation of, 124, 127
   offense of, 116
   presumption of, 122
   of privilege, 110, 119–121,
      126–128, 130–131
   reconsideration of, 125
   of representation, 123
   significance of, 120
single-parent household, 171
Sisters of Charity, 90, 94–97
sixties, the, 4
slave trade, 29
slavery, 28, 30, 75
slaves, 29, 74, 75
Smith, Barbara Herrnstein, 26
social injustice, 156, 158
social justice, 15, 22, 90, 92,
   99–100, 152, 165
social studies, 144
Social Text (journal), 150
social theory, 127

society, good, 20
Socrates, 35, 70
Sokal, Alan D., 150
Sony, 85
Spanish, 73, 84
spelling, 84
spiritual revolution, 32
Spivak, Gayatri, 81
split infinitive, 78
St. Ignatius Loyola grammar
   school, 113
standard English, 11–12, 60,
   66–70, 72–73, 75–76, 78–
   80, 84, 87, 138, 169
   attitudes toward, 67–69
   benefits of, 12, 66
   correctness of, 80, 84
   debate, 78
   democracy, 12
   development of, 79
   domination by, 80
   historic context, 73
   history of, 79
   justification for, 67–68
   linguistic value, 72
   morality of, 12, 68, 79
   non-linguistic factors, 12
   pragmatism of, 68, 79
   rejection of, 138
   resisting, 73
   v. substandard English, 66–67
   superiority of, 68
   teaching, 75
stories, 161–165
   of gods, 161–163
straight, 109–110, 118. *See also*
   gays; heterosexual privilege
*Straight No Chaser: How I
   Became a Grown-up Black
   Woman* (Nelson)
strategies
   education, 69, 138
   of repetition, 124
   of self-exploration, 128
Stuart, Mary C., 96

student(s). *See also* African-
American; Hispanics
African American, 77
of color, 10, 42, 66–67, 138
recruitment, 97
teaching, 65–66
urban, 65–66
substandard English, 11–12, 66,
86
survival, 70–71

*Talking Power: The Politics of
Language* (Lakoff), 69
Taylor, Charles, 155
Teacher Center. *See* New York
City Teacher Center
Teachers College at Columbia
University, 51
teachers of color, 62
teachers. *See* educators
teaching, 3–4, 7–11, 15–16, 31,
37–39
age of uncertainty and, 31,
37, 39
complexities of, 42
curriculum, 97
as dialogue, 176
ethical positions and, 16
extra-moral, 15, 166–168,
170, 172, 174, 176
history, 30
moral principles, 15
practices, 125
science, 148
standard English, 75
tolerance, 166
to transgress, 38–39, 166–167
unchartered territory and, 39
unspeakable dimension of, 118
urban, 42, 90
*Teaching to Transgress: Education
as the Practice of Freedom*
(hooks), 167
techniques of self, 120–122, 130
Temple University, 141

tenure, 118
"The Prescriptive Tradition"
(Crystal essay), 80
theater, 129
theatrical exercises, 130
theatrical language, 130
*Theorizing Multiculturalism: A
Guide to the Current Debate*
(Willett), 153–154
tobacco advertisements, 163
tolerance, 158
Tower of Babel, 70
Townsend Harris High School,
90–91
traditional history, 25–26
democracy and, 26
traditionalists, 28–29, 165
traditions, 86
agricultural, 148
astronomical, 148
biological, 148
"Transformative Hermeneutics
of Quantum Gravity" (Sokal
article), 150
transient, 74
transracial communication, 141
trust, 42
truth, 15, 20, 22–25, 28, 30–33,
38–40, 126, 166
democratic society and, 38
as experience, 126
historical, 30, 37
lies and, 25, 40
loss of, 20, 23
new rules for, 32
political system and, 25
religious right and, 38
respecting, 25, 29
truth telling, 10, 25, 29, 39
Tubertini, Barbara, 101–105, 107
*Twilight Zones: The Hidden Life
of Cultural Images from Plato to
O.J.* (Bordo), 48
Uncommon Differences (Kohl),
29–30

undergraduate students, 96
United Federation of Teachers,
 51, 101
United States, 73, 137, 142,
 164–165, 174–175
 history, 29–30, 137, 142,
 164–165, 175
 myth, 30
urban education, 13, 42, 65, 67,
 92, 98–99

value(s), 1– 5, 9–10, 15, 22, 38,
 131, 158–159, 164–175
 Anglo-Christian, 164–165
 Christian, 159
 of culture, 158–159
 debate on, 1–5, 22
 deconstruction of, 21
 deconstructive, 170
 definition of, 169–170
 democratic, 131
 extra-moral, 15
 family, 2, 38, 166, 170–175
 identity and, 172–173
 as meaning, 169–170
 promoting *v.* demanding, 172
 reconstruction of, 21
 relation and, 173
 static, 171
 as status, 169–170
Vazquez, Felix, 42, 51

We Are All Multiculturists Now
 (Glazer), 133–136
wedding ring, 109–111,
 119–120, 131
 symbol, 111
West, Cornel, 6, 23–24, 32–33
Western culture, 144
Western science, 147
Western tradition, 9–10, 27, 70,
 148–149
white(s), 45, 53, 63, 73, 118,
 122, 136–137
 community, 53, 136
 culture, 73, 122
 guilt, 137
 intervention, 45
 supremist, 63
Wilfork, John Noble, 71
Willett, Cynthia, 153–155
women
 abuse of, 158
 sexualizing, 48
 status of, 37, 44
world music concerts, 157

Yale Law School, 112, 114
Yale University, 112
yeshiva, 91
Yonkers, 95, 97
Yoshida, Roland, 93, 100
youth, 161